ACTIVITIES TO DEVELOP LEARNING SKILLS AT KS4

Helen Sonnet and Cassandra Sonnet

Permission to photocopy

This book contains materials which may be reproduced by photocopier or other means for use by the purchaser. The permission is granted on the understanding that these copies will be used within the educational establishment of the purchaser. The book and all its contents remain copyright. Copies may be made without reference to the publisher or the licensing scheme for the making of photocopies operated by the Publishers Licensing Agency.

The rights of Helen Sonnet and Cassandra Sonnet to be identified as the authors of this work have been asserted by them in accordance with sections 77 and 78 of the Copyright, Designs and Patents Act.

Activities to Develop Learning Skills at KS4
ISBN: 978-1-85503-529-4

© Helen Sonnet and Cassandra Sonnet
Illustrations by Bethan Matthews and Tony Forbes/Sylvie Poggio Artists
(Bethan Matthews: pp. 139, 144, 146, 151; Tony Forbes: pp. 138, 141–143, 145)

All rights reserved
First published 2012
Printed in the UK for LDA
LDA, Findel Education, Hyde Buildings, Ashton Road, Hyde, Cheshire, SK14 4SH

Contents

CONTENTS

INTRODUCTION

The importance of learning skills

As any Key Stage 4 teacher will know, the race to teach the vast swathes of the curriculum can, all too often, impact upon the holistic idea of teaching *how* to learn: in other words, imparting those skills we need in order to understand, analyse and evaluate information.

Schools are like pressure cookers, steaming towards exam success, and teachers can feel that devoting any lesson time to something that is not going to be examined explicitly is a waste of time and energy.

Even the most conscientious and diligent teachers, who understand the intrinsic value of teaching learning skills, may be unable to devote adequate time to such activities for fear of missing out on valuable curriculum time. It may appear pointless to spend a few hours on teaching *how* to analyse rather than *what* to analyse and, at Key Stage 4 level in particular, talking-led activities without a written outcome or with deviations from the prescribed lesson plans and schemes of work may appear to be of little value. Yet this reluctance to enable students to become aware of their own 'learning skills' could be hindering them from reaching or, indeed, surpassing their target grades.

In many subjects, there is a sliding scale of independent thinking that corresponds to grade outcomes from, broadly speaking, 'awareness' at one end to 'originality of analysis' at the other. However, many students do not know the difference between, for example, insight and originality of analysis, and this is where movement up to the next grade may be hindered.

Teachers sometimes expect students automatically to know and understand the differences, but many students may never have been taught these skills explicitly. For example, pupils in an English class studying *Romeo and Juliet* may have considerable difficulty in formulating their own response to the character of Juliet. They may have little strength in their own convictions, lack confidence in their ability to think analytically, or even fail to realise that they are being asked to make a personal interpretation of the play. More importantly, they can be unaware that they will be rewarded if they do so. All too often, students think that the examiner wants to read what Shakespeare or 'Miss' believe and do not realise that they are not simply vessels that knowledge is poured into in the classroom, in order to seep out again in the exam hall. Students need to grasp that they are being 'allowed' to make personal judgements on this knowledge. This is what is really meant by 'independence of learning'.

A knowledge of metacognition can actually save time in the long run. Taking a ten-minute break from teaching curriculum information in order to engage in a designated activity instead can illustrate, for example, *how* to interpret and exactly what interpretation is and means. Once students are confident in their understanding of a skill they can transfer this ability back to the curriculum. Pupils who may have little awareness of how to offer personal opinions on a poem may have no hesitation in offering their views on fashion, football or an *X Factor* contestant. Once they realise that skills are transferable and that their personal opinions are relevant in response to curriculum stimulation, students are much less hesitant to offer their own responses.

Awareness of the skills needed for certain grades is also fundamental to a cross-curricular, whole school ethos. With the grind of teaching and pastoral roles pressing on a teacher, it can be difficult to see how teaching in one department can help in another. However, this is to miss a significant method in raising whole school attainment. Schools aim to help students move towards ownership of their individual learning through both reflective and target-setting episodes. If these occur consistently over many different subjects, a cross-curricular approach will raise standards through a student's self-awareness and their ability to set meaningful targets. If, for example, a student's target grade is 'C', they are more likely to achieve this if they are made aware of the skills needed to answer exam questions thoroughly or to complete course work accurately, at the required level, rather than simply being familiar with curriculum content.

The activities in this book aim to develop a greater awareness in students of how to achieve their target grades. They do this through offering fun, exciting and motivational introductions to the method of exploring the curriculum that each grade requires. The headings are not concrete grade descriptors for all subjects and, although the sections are ordered in progression of independence of thinking, there is some overlapping as one skill may require the mastery of another to successfully complete a task. Skills such as insight and interpretation are similar and so when a student can achieve the first, they can very easily manage the second.

Some of the activities in this book lend themselves to quick ten-minute intervals within lessons, while others may take a whole lesson or parts of several lessons to complete. A rough guideline of time is given with each activity, but this does not include the extension. The activities could also be used in the pastoral tutor programmes in schools, especially during the run up to examinations or revision time-tabling.

The move away from basic retention of taught material towards an analytical, evaluative approach is a positive and enabling step for students to take. Even those students who are unlikely to achieve the higher grades will become more engaged in school life when they realise that the personal skills that they possess are valued within the classroom, making school appear to be 'less difficult'. The activities in this book will not prompt the response 'Can't do that, Miss, it's too hard'.

The skill-enhancing activities aim to prepare students for the world outside school as well as to promote self-awareness, confidence and independence. Students who take ownership of their own learning and education are much more likely to achieve the five outcomes set out in the document *Every Child Matters: Change for Children* (DfES 2004) and enjoy personal and social development, make a positive contribution, successfully deal with significant life changes and develop enterprising behaviour.

Not only will the activities in this book develop valuable learning skills, they will create opportunities within the classroom for fun and enjoyment!

AWARENESS

Awareness is the ability of a pupil to draw on their inherent knowledge of a subject, prior to explicit teaching. It proves to a pupil that they know things already, highlighting the fact that they are able to retain information and therefore can be taught. Teaching 'awareness' is particularly helpful to disaffected pupils who see no value in learning, or those who have self-esteem issues and feel they 'can't do it'. It demonstrates that they do have the ability to learn and, therefore, can learn within the school environment.

True or False

This activity is a straightforward example of awareness of detail in relayed information.

Group size: Individual

Time: 15–20 minutes

Resources: Paper and pencils

What to do

Read the text below to the students and then read the following statements. The students must decide whether each statement is true (T) or false (F) and write down their answers.

'In my line of business it's the detail that counts. I'm a secret agent, known to my bosses as 008. At the moment I'm staking out a warehouse, where a known terrorist is waiting to meet his contact. I'm here to discover the identity of that contact. It's 5.30 p.m. and busy with people leaving work. There are two stationary cars in front of the building, one a red sporty number. A man approaches the warehouse. He is tall, with a beard and wearing a black jacket and grey trousers. He stops by the entrance, but then bends down to tie a shoe-lace. He moves on. An elderly woman comes next. She is wearing a brown coat and pulling a tartan shopping trolley. Unlikely, but you never know. She shuffles past without stopping. A young woman in training gear runs up the road. Her vest top is wet with sweat. She does not slow down. Next up is a bloke. Late thirties, I'd say, bald, a bit paunchy, scruffy denim jacket, folded newspaper under his right arm. He is looking around him, suspicious, I think, but he walks on. A smart lady with a small poodle comes next. Grey pin-striped suit, black high-heeled shoes, carrying a triangular-shaped bag. Not very likely to be the contact, I think. I am about to look away from her, when she slows and bends down. In one quick movement, she scoops up her small dog, turns on her heel and enters the building. I have my suspect. Just goes to show that appearances can be deceiving.'

Questions

Write T (True) or F (False) for each statement. Number each answer.

1. The secret agent said that it was the 'detail' that counted in his line of business. (T)

2. He is known as 009 to his bosses. (F)

3. He was watching a factory. (F)

4. He was trying to discover the identity of a known terrorist. (F)

5. It was 5.30 p.m. (T)

6. There were three cars parked outside the building. (F)

7. The sports car was green. (F)

8. The first man to approach the building was tall. (T)

9. He was wearing grey trousers. (T)

10. He bent down to pick up a coin. (F)

11. The elderly lady was pulling a brown shopping trolley. (F)

12. The next person was a man running. (F)

13. The runner was wearing a vest top. (T)

14. The second man had a beard. (F)

15. He was in his late thirties. (T)

16. He carried a magazine under his right arm. (F)

17. The smart lady had a poodle. (T)

18. She was wearing a grey check suit. (F)

19. Her handbag was triangular in shape. (T)

20. The secret agent said, 'Appearances can be revealing.' (F)

Extension

Depending on the ability of your group, you can ask the students individually or in pairs to write their own text with 20 true or false statements.

What makes a rainbow?

This activity demonstrates to students that they have an understanding and awareness of things and encourages them to be explicit in their explanations.

Group size: 6+

Time: 20–30 minutes

Resources: Paper and pencils; for each group, a copy of photocopiable sheet *What makes a rainbow?* (p. 123)

What to do

Put the students into evenly matched groups of six or more. Give each group a photocopy of the questions to answer. Allow a set time, then call the groups together to mark their answers. Discuss with the students how they pick up information and details about the world around them without conscious effort.

Extension

Ask each group to think of five similar questions that they can ask the other groups.

Why are things ...?

This activity encourages the students to show an awareness of what things are and to extend their knowledge with explanations.

Group size: 4+

Time: 20 minutes

Resources: Paper and pencils

What to do

Put the students into evenly matched groups. Ask them to think of ten things that are round and the reason why. (For example a wheel or ball is round so it can roll, the rim of a cup is round to aid drinking.) Next ask them to think of ten things that are red and the reasons why. (For example a red traffic light is bright red to show danger, and a red heart is the colour of blood to show love.) In some cases there may not be one specific answer; it is enough that the students think of viable explanations.

Extension

Ask the students to make up a 'red' item with a suitable explanation for its colour, for example a red love potion, or a red seat to encourage romance.

What am I?

This activity facilitates the idea that people have a shared awareness of things.

Group size: 3–4

Time: 20–30 minutes

Resources: Paper and pencils

What to do

Put the students into small groups. Explain that they are going to choose an object or animal and write five statements about it. The statements must be on an ascending scale of information about their object. For example, if the object was a watering can, the statements could be:

1. I am used in the garden.

2. I am usually green.

3. I am mostly used in the summer.

4. I am especially useful when it is hot and sunny.

5. I have a handle and a spout for pouring.

They read their statements, one at a time, for another team to guess. The second team can confer, but they only have one official guess per statement. Points are awarded on a descending scale, i.e. 5 points for a correct guess after the first statement, 4 points for a guess after the second statement and so on. Discuss with the students how they all knew certain facts about each item. Where do they think the common knowledge comes from?

Variation

The students could repeat this game using 'Leisure Activities' as their topic.

A shark is a great hunter because ...

This activity demonstrates awareness that many factors can contribute to and be influential in the same category.

Group size: Pairs or groups of 3–4

Time: 15–20 minutes

Resources: Paper and pencils

What to do

Put the students into pairs or small groups. Ask them to complete the following sentence stems. They must think of the attributes that are relevant to each animal:

- A shark is a great hunter because ...
- A tiger is a great hunter because ...
- An eagle is a great hunter because ...
- A cheetah is a great hunter because ...
- A python is a great hunter because ...

Encourage the students to understand that there are various different attributes that can make an animal a good hunter. For example, a tiger is a great hunter because it has stripes to camouflage it while it stalks its prey; a cheetah is a great hunter because it can run fast; an eagle is a great hunter because it has sharp talons to catch its prey.

Other categories could be:

- A rabbit (dog, cat, hamster, budgerigar) is a great pet because ...
- (Name five bands) is a great band because ...
- (Name five footballers who play in different positions) is a great footballer because ...

Extension

Ask each pair/group to think of a category with five named contributors. If you think they will find this difficult, you could make a list on the board of their suggestions and then ask each group to choose a category from the list.

Who would advertise your product?

This activity encourages awareness of influential factors, as the students have to think of several different aspects for their products.

 Group size: Pairs or groups of 3–4

 Time: 30–40 minutes

 Resources: Paper and pencils

What to do

Put the students into pairs or small groups and write the following list on the board: trainers, perfume, a non-alcoholic drink for teenagers, an electronic game. Explain that they are going to select one of the products listed and then choose a current celebrity to advertise their product. They must consider the target customer and what type of celebrity would appeal to them. They must also plan their advertising campaign and describe what would be involved, for example magazine advertisements, television advertisements, billboards.

Variation

Ask the students to make up their own product. They can use their imaginations to design an item creatively, even if it is unrealistic.

What am I saying ...?

This activity demonstrates a shared awareness about things.

 Group size: Pairs or groups of 3–4

 Time: 20–30 minutes

 Resources: Paper and pencils

What to do

Put the students into pairs or small groups. Explain that they must write down a statement, for example: 'I am hungry', 'I want to watch the television', 'I need some money', 'I need to put on sun-cream'. They must think of sentences about their statement that express the same meaning obliquely, without referring directly to the content of their statement. For example, if the statement was 'I am hungry', they might say, 'Nothing has passed my lips for four hours' or 'My stomach is making a strange noise.' The groups say the sentences, one at a time, to another group or the whole class, allowing a guess between each sentence. The other students must guess the exact wording of the original sentence. Ask the students what helped them to guess the answers correctly – that is, a common knowledge that all people share.

Variation

The students must mime, rather than speak, their sentences.

Ingredients

This activity demonstrates an awareness of categorisation.

Group size: Individual

Time: 10 minutes

Resources: Make one copy of photocopiable sheet *Ingredients* (p. 124) and cut out the individual cards. There are five cards giving the names of types of dishes (categories), each with five ingredients. For lower ability groups, colour each category card so that they are clearly visible, while leaving the ingredients card plain. If you laminate the cards, they can be used repeatedly.

What to do

Hand out the category and ingredients cards, one per student and face down. Tell the students that the activity involves various dishes and their ingredients. You might want to give an example of a dish not included. Explain that on your command 'Go!' they must turn over their cards and find the correct category for their ingredient. They do this by asking other students which ingredients they have, and grouping themselves accordingly. They can stick the category cards on the wall or place them on tables and each student with an ingredient stands by the relevant one. Tell the students that each category card has five ingredients. If you wish, you can set a time limit for the activity. When the sets have been completed, collect in the cards, shuffle them and repeat.

Variation

You can make your own sets of cards with different categories. For example the categories could be lessons and the ingredients could be words used in those lessons. You can make the 'ingredients' easier or more difficult depending on the age and ability of the group.

Category: History. **Ingredients:** Romans, Iron Age, Tudor, World War 1, Domesday Book.

Category: Biology. **Ingredients:** amoeba, digestive system, photosynthesis, pulmonary artery, gene.

Who's the tallest?

This activity demonstrates innate awareness to the students. They hold information in their brains that has been gathered without conscious effort.

 Group size: 10

 Time: 20–25 minutes

 Resources: Paper and pencils

What to do

Put the students into two or three groups. Tell them to make a quick list of everyone in their group. Ask them to sit down in a circle facing outwards. Explain that they are going to write down the names of everyone in their group in order of height, from the shortest to the tallest. They must not stand up nor must they turn round to look at the other members of their group. They must complete this activity using the information stored in their brains. Allow a set time and then call the groups together. Ask each group to stand in line in order of height to see how accurate their lists are. Discuss with the students the factors that helped them to complete this activity.

Variation

Ask the students to write down from memory the names of everyone in their class in the order that they appear in the register. Allow a limited time for this so that the students can't look around and work out the order alphabetically. The object of the activity is to show the students that they assimilate information without conscious effort.

Can you draw a ...?

This activity demonstrates that people have a shared awareness of conventions.

 Group size: Individual

Time: 20–30 minutes

Resources: Paper and pencils

What to do

Give each student a pencil and paper and ask them to draw a vampire and label the special characteristics that identify it. Ask the students to try not to look at anyone else's drawing while they are doing this, because you want to compare their interpretations. Allow a set time, around ten minutes, for them to complete this task. Ask for volunteers to each name one characteristic they have drawn and tell the other students to make a tick if they have the same characteristic. Discuss with the students how similar their drawings were and how people have a shared awareness of conventions. Other items you could draw are a clown, a castle or a sports car.

Variation

With higher attaining students, you might want to ask for a written, rather than a drawn, description.

Fantasy crisps

This activity demonstrates people's shared awareness of common food pairings.

Group size: Individual

Time: 15–20 minutes

Resources: Paper and pencils

What to do

Give each student a piece of paper and a pencil. Explain that they are going to invent a series of fantasy crisp flavours. Each flavour has two ingredients. You will supply one and the students must provide a second appropriate ingredient. Remind them of current popular flavours such as salt and vinegar and cheese and onion. Either write on the board or call out the following:

Bacon and …   Horse radish sauce and ….
Mint sauce and …   Jelly and …
Peanut butter and …   Sausage and …
Fish and …   Toasty soldiers and …
Apple pie and …   Pickle and …

Compare how many 'matches' there are for each combination. Ask the students why so many of them chose the same second ingredient.

Extension

Put the students into groups of five or six and ask them to think of other common food combinations. They can then test other groups, by giving them one of each combination and asking them to supply the second ingredient.

One-liners

This activity demonstrates to the students their awareness of shared experiences.

Group size: Individual

Time: 10–15 minutes

Resources: None

What to do

Explain to the students that they are going to think of one line of speech from a situation. For example: 'Open wide' from a visit to the dentist, 'Salt or vinegar?' at a fish and chip shop, 'Single to Bath, please' at the railway station, 'How much shall I cut off?' at the hairdressers. Ask for volunteers to say their line and then invite the other students to guess the situation. Discuss with the students how they were able to guess the context from just one line.

Variation

Ask the students to mime an action from a situation for the others to guess.

Stages of life

This activity demonstrates the students' common awareness of the features of the different stages of life.

Group size: Pairs

Time: 20–30 minutes

Resources: Paper and pencils; for each pair, a copy of photocopiable sheet *Stages of life* (p. 125), which contains Jaques' speech 'All the world's a stage' from Act II, Scene VII of William Shakespeare's play *As You Like It.*

What to do

Read the speech 'All the world's a stage' by William Shakespeare to the students and explain any vocabulary that they don't understand. Explain that this was written in the 16th century, when most people received no education, life expectancy was much shorter and medicine rudimentary. In pairs, ask them to write down all the stages of life that they can think of that are relevant to today. Discuss the stages to identify those that are most commonly recognised by all the students.

Extension

Write several life stages on the board, for example baby, toddler, teenager, old person. Ask each pair to choose two from the list and write down the characteristics of that particular life stage. Compare the common features from each stage.

Fish or fowl?

This activity demonstrates to the students that they have a shared awareness of different life forms.

 Group size: Individual

 Time: 15–20 minutes

 Resources: Paper and pencils

What to do

Ask the students to write at the top of their paper the headings: plant, fish, bird, reptile and mammal. Call out the following numbered words, asking the students to simply write the corresponding number under the correct heading. It may fit into more than one heading. Call the words out quite rapidly so that the students have to respond quickly.

1. beak	10. cold-blooded	19. roe
2. fin	11. talon	20. spawn
3. scales	12. nest	21. birth
4. milk	13. glide	22. constrictor
5. root	14. warm-blooded	23. wing
6. claw	15. thorn	24. mammary gland
7. fur	16. chlorophyll	25. forked tongue.
8. petal	17. bud	
9. gill	18. shoal	

Go through the list of words and ask the students to volunteer answers. Did they all agree on the relevant headings?

Extension

Ask the students to think of as many additional words as possible that correspond with each heading.

Time-line

This activity shows the students that they have an innate awareness of historical context.

Group size: 3–4

Time: 15–20 minutes

Resources: Collect a series of pictures of moments in history and copy a set for each group

What to do

Put the students into groups and give each group a set of the pictures you have prepared. Ask the students to put the pictures into chronological order, starting with the earliest and ending with the most recent. Discuss with the students the visual clues that helped them to decide on the order, such as costumes, buildings, vehicles. Ask the students if they were surprised by the amount of knowledge they had that helped them to work out a time-line.

Variation

You can make this a whole class exercise by putting the students into pairs and giving each pair a picture. The students must use the visual clues to put themselves into a time-line.

FAMILIARITY

Familiarity demonstrates the ability to develop basic retention of taught material. It is the first step towards engagement and a personal response to a subject. The activities in this section may be particularly helpful in boosting confidence for those students who are struggling with more advanced thinking.

Hand clap

This activity uses hand-clapping patterns to produce memorable lines.

 Group size: 4

 Time: 15–20 minutes

 Resources: Paper and pencils

What to do

Put the students into groups of four and number them from 1 to 4 within their groups. Prior to the lesson, work out four lines of hand-clapping rhythms, for example:

1. Slow slow quick-quick slow

2. Slow quick-quick slow quick-quick

3. Quick-quick quick-quick slow slow

4. Slow quick-quick quick-quick slow.

Ask all the number 1 students to come out to you. Teach them the first line of the clapping rhythm and then instruct them to go back to their groups and teach the other three members this line. Repeat with the number 2, 3 and 4 students and the next three clapping lines. Finally ask the groups to clap through all four lines one after the other and clap through with them.

Extension

Let each group make up their own four-line clapping rhythm and teach it in the same way, line by line, to the students of the other groups. They can write their lines down on paper to help them remember if they need to.

We're the same

This activity focuses the students' attention, as they need to remember other students who choose the same category.

 Group size: Individual

 Time: 15–20 minutes

 Resources: Whiteboard and pen

What to do

Write six popular drinks on the board, for example cola, lemonade, milk, orange juice, apple juice, water. Ask the students to say, just once, and in quick succession, their favourite drink from the list. Instruct the students to silently get into groups of like-minded people, that is, all those who chose the same drink. Allow them one minute then call 'stop' and see how successful they have been in remembering who chose what. Repeat with another list of six, such as chocolate bars, dinners, films, pop groups. Were they more successful the second time and, if so, why do they think that is?

Variation

Repeat the activity, but after each round ask the students to write down all the other people who chose the same as they did, rather than move into the groups physically.

Copy the pattern

The object of this activity is for students to retain and reproduce the visual pattern created by shapes.

Group size: Pairs or groups of 3–4

Time: 20–30 minutes

Resources: For each group, a copy of photocopiable sheet *Shapes* (p. 126), plain paper, pencils and an extra sheet of paper to cover the patterns they are going to make

What to do

Put the students into pairs or small groups, giving each set a sheet of the photocopied shapes to cut out. The students take turns to create a pattern on the plain paper using the cut-out shapes. They show the pattern to their partner/group for one minute, then place a cover over the pattern. The other members of the group try to draw the pattern on a piece of paper. Allow a set time for this, then let the students compare their drawings with the original pattern. It might be wise to advise low attainment students to start with no more than six shapes.

Variation

Ask the students to draw six rectangles each 8cm by 2cm and shade each rectangle in a different colour. They cut each rectangle into four equal parts (2cm by 2cm). The students take turns to create a pattern of coloured shapes and repeat the procedure above.

Crack the code

In this activity, the students are required to retain information that they have been shown, in order to write and decipher messages in code.

Group size: Individual

Time: 20–30 minutes

Resources: Whiteboard and pen; paper and pencils

What to do

Write a word on the board with a code underneath. Two examples are given below, the first for lower and the second for higher attainers.

S	A	T	U	R	D	A	Y
1	2	3	4	5	6	2	7

R	E	F	U	R	B	I	S	H	M	E	N	T
1	2	3	4	1	5	6	7	8	9	2	10	11

Allow the students to study the word and its code for one minute, then cover up the word. Ask them to make as many words of three letters or more as they can from the given word, and write the words in code. When they have completed this, instruct them to swap papers with another student to decode the words that they have written.

Extension

Write another long word on the board, but use letters rather than numbers in the code to make the task more difficult.

What's been added?

In this activity, the students are required to study and memorise a pattern in order to discover which new lines have been added.

Group size: Individual

Time: 5 minutes

Resources: A photocopy, enlarged to fill A3 paper, of the photocopiable sheet *What's been added?* (p. 127), and a black pen the same thickness as the lines in the pattern

What to do

At the start of a lesson, display the line pattern for all the students to see. Explain that they need to study the pattern closely as you will add a small detail before each lesson for them to find. You can make the detail smaller or more visible depending on the ability of the group to spot the addition.

Variation

Photocopy a page of factual, descriptive text for the students to study. Each week change a word in the text for them to spot.

Follow my instructions

The students have to listen carefully and remember a set of instructions that they must then follow.

 Group size: Individual

 Time: 10 minutes

 Resources: Paper and pencils

What to do

Read a set of instructions to the students while they listen. When you have finished speaking, ask the students to carry out your instructions. The number of instructions you give will depend on the age and ability of your students, but start with three as a minimum. An example of instructions is given below.

 Draw a circle in the centre of your page, drop a line down from the circle to the bottom of the page, place a cross in the top right hand corner, draw a box around the circle in the centre, put a tick in the bottom left hand corner, draw a diagonal line from the cross to the tick, write the letter 'N' directly above the circle.

Extension

Add colours to your instructions. So, for example, ask the students to draw a red box or a green cross. To make it more confusing, ask the students to write the word 'red' in yellow.

A day to remember

The students must listen to the extract carefully in order to recall details of information.

 Group size: Individual

 Time: 20–30 minutes

 Resources: Paper and pencils

What to do

Explain to the students that you will read them an extract, after which you will ask them questions about the details mentioned. Read one of the extracts below according to the level of attainment of your students.

Low attainment

'Saturday started well. The sun was shining when I got up at 8 o'clock. I had a quick shower and got dressed, then made some porridge for my breakfast. I had to meet my two friends Joe and Amir at 9 o'clock outside Burger King. We were going to look around the shops together. Joe bought a new sweatshirt and some Nike trainers. We spent a long time looking at games for my PS2 and I bought a sci fi game that looked really exciting. Amir spent ages going in every clothes shop there was looking for a new jacket but he couldn't find anything that he liked. We went into McDonalds where Joe and I had cheeseburgers and chips, but Amir had a veggieburger.'

Questions

1. What day was it?

2. What was the weather like?

3. At what time did the writer get up?

4. What did the writer have for breakfast?

5. Name one of the writer's friends.

6. Where was the writer meeting his friends?

7. At what time did the writer have to meet his friends?

8. What make of trainers did Joe buy?

9. What PS2 game did the writer buy?

10. Who had the veggieburger in McDonalds?

High attainment

'Saturday started well. The sun was shining when I crawled out of bed at 7.30 a.m. I had a quick shower and dressed, putting on an extra pair of socks for comfort, then grabbed my packed lunch from the fridge. I was meeting the other three in front of Burger King and they were already there by the time I arrived. We planned to walk 12 miles along the coastal path with a stop for lunch at 12.30 then catch the 'Rover' bus back. I reckoned the walk would take around four and a half hours with a lunch break of half an hour or so. We were soon into a steady walking rhythm. I brought up the rear, Joe led, Zac was behind him and Rory in front of me. The scenery was spectacular and there was plenty of wildlife to watch. We even saw a red kite circling above us in the sunlight and watched six yachts in a race.

The path was hard going, with many steep ascents and descents, so I was glad of the rest when we stopped for lunch. I swapped one of my peanut butter sandwiches for one of Zac's tuna rolls, which added a nice touch of variety, and thirstily drank the blackcurrant squash I had packed. We were all a bit reluctant to set off again after our stop, but once we got going we were O.K. We were probably about a mile from our destination, when disaster struck. Joe slipped on a particularly steep step and badly twisted his ankle. Luckily, Rory had a first aid kit in his rucksack and was able to strap Joe's ankle up for him and give him a couple of paracetamol for the pain, but even so our progress was seriously slowed as we had to help him on the trickier sections of the path. The hold-up meant that we missed the bus connection we were aiming for and had to wait 45 minutes for the next bus. In spite of this we had enjoyed our outing and Joe proposed that we repeat the walk in the autumn.

Questions

1. On which day did the walk take place?

2. At what time did the writer get out of bed?

3. What extra clothing did the writer put on?

4. How many boys were walking altogether?

5. What distance did they plan to walk?

6. What time did they plan to stop for lunch?

7. What was the name of the bus that they were intending to catch back?

8. How long did the writer think that the walk would take?

9. Who was third in line during the walk?

10. What type of bird did the writer mention?

11. How many yachts were racing?

12. Who had brought tuna rolls for lunch?

13. What did the writer have in his sandwiches?

14. How far from the end of the walk were they when Joe twisted his ankle?

15. Who had a first aid kit in his rucksack?

16. What did Joe take for the pain?

17. How long did the boys have to wait for a bus?

18. When did Joe suggest that they walk again?

I see, I hear, I say, I smell

This activity encourages the students to retain and compartmentalise taught material.

Group size: Individual

Time: 20–30 minutes

Resources: Paper and pencils

What to do

Ask the students to draw a basic head on their paper with eyes, ears, nose and mouth. Explain that you will read a passage, at the end of which they must write down what the narrator saw (next to the eyes), heard (next to the ears), smelled (next to the nose) and tasted (by the mouth).

'I walked in a forest on a late summer's day. The brilliant green of the leaves was dazzling, though the ground was dry and dusty. The calls of many birds echoed around me and in the distance a cow mooed and a tractor hummed. Above me the sky was clear and blue. Pale, yellow butterflies flitted from bush to bush among the sweet scented flowers. The wind whistled through the trees, causing the leaves to rustle on the branches. I reached out for a blackberry and popped the purple fruit into my mouth. I came upon the remains of a dead rabbit. Flies buzzed hungrily about it and its foul odour wafted up to my nose. The unpleasant smell penetrated my nostrils so that I could taste the scent on my tongue. I turned quickly and walked away towards the entrance. I could hear the voices of people in the café and as I got closer I could smell the welcome smell of food cooking. I sat in the café and enjoyed a cup of tea and slice of fruit cake.'

Extension

Ask the students to draw a complete body and add feelings next to the torso (for example, I felt happy, scared, thirsty) and body movements next to the limbs (for example, I walked, ran, felt tired, touched).

In my garden I have ...

This activity encourages students to focus their attention in order to remember all the items that have been mentioned.

 Group size: 5 (low attainment) or 10 (high attainment)

 Time: 30+ minutes

 Resources: Paper and pencils

What to do

Put the students into groups of five (low attainment) or ten (high attainment). Each student in the group needs to think of a feature that could go into a garden and complete the sentence stem 'In my garden I have ...' For example: 'In my garden I have a bird table/red rose/round pond/plum tree/lawn'. The students take turns in their groups to say their sentence. If the object they chose has already been said, they need to think of a different one. When everyone in the group has spoken, the students must draw the garden including all the items mentioned. They are not allowed to ask for reminders.

Variation

Other sentence stems that could be used are: 'In my fridge I have a ...', 'In my wardrobe I have a ...' and 'In my house I have a ...'

Match the words

This activity aims to demonstrate to the students that they have learned familiar words relating to certain events.

Group size: 6

Time: 20–30 minutes

Resources: Paper and pencils

What to do

Put the students into groups of six and ask them to number themselves 1–6. Explain that you will write a word on the board. Without conferring, they must each write down six words (or fewer for lower attaining groups) that they associate with the word written on the board. When everyone has completed this, the number 1 in each group reads out their list of words. If the numbers 2–6 have the same words written in their list they award themselves a point for each corresponding word. The activity continues in this way with the number 2 students reading out their list for the second word, number 3s for the third and so on. At the end each student totals their points and then makes a combined total for their group. Examples of words are:

1. Christmas

4. Holiday

2. Spring

5. Olympics

3. Birthday

6. Easter

Variation

This activity can be made subject specific, although you might ask for fewer words. For example, for biology you might use such words as internal organs, animal groups or plant structure.

All about me

Students are required to remember facts about their classmates in this activity.

Group size: Individual

Time: 30+ minutes

Resources: Paper and pencils

What to do

Depending on the attainment level of your students, ask them to write down five to ten facts about themselves. For lower attaining students you might want to put up five categories, such as favourite dinner, favourite film, favourite animal, favourite subject in school, favourite chocolate bar. For higher attaining students, you could let them choose random facts about themselves. When everyone has completed this, call out five students and ask them, in turn, to say all of their chosen facts. Make a note of their responses or ask for their written list of facts. When all five students have spoken, ask questions relating to the given facts for the other students to answer. They can either do this verbally or give written responses. You can either give the fact and ask which student it relates to or ask for a particular student's favourite item.

Variation

Create a set of between six and ten fictitious characters with their food preferences, for example: the tall man likes pizza, the red-haired girl likes fish and chips, the old lady likes chicken and chips. Read out the characters and their food preferences to the students, then choose three who visit a restaurant and ask the students what they would order to eat.

I'm afraid of ...

The aim of this activity is to encourage students to compartmentalise in their heads and then recall the facts.

Group size: Individual

Time: 15–20 minutes

Resources: Whiteboard and pen

What to do

Write up three to six (depending on the attainment level of your students) items on the board that are common 'fears', for example spiders, snakes, rats, the dark, ghosts, being confined in small spaces. Ask the students to look at the list and decide which item they would most fear. Ask for a show of hands for each item and count them out loud. After you have completed the list ask the students to see if they can remember how many voted for each item. Could anyone correctly remember the numbers for all six items?

Variation

You could repeat this activity replacing 'fears' with the most hated vegetable, using brussel sprouts, carrots, broccoli, cabbage, courgettes, onions.

Cartoon sequence

The students listen to a text and then reproduce the sequence of events from memory in cartoon form.

 Group size: Individual

 Time: 20–30 minutes

 Resources: Paper and pencils

What to do

The students prepare a series of boxes (five to ten, depending on their attainment level) on their paper to represent a cartoon strip. Read the text below (use the first half only for lower attaining students and both halves for higher attaining students) then ask the students to draw the events for their cartoon character in the correct sequence that you have read to them. They don't have to record Gianni's movements from room to room.

Gianni got up and went into the bathroom. He cleaned his teeth and went back into the bedroom and put on his trousers and jumper. Downstairs in the kitchen, he couldn't make his mind up what to have for breakfast, but eventually decided on cereal, then he sat on a stool by the kitchen table to eat. He had an hour before he was meeting his friend so he passed the time by playing on his PS2.

He slipped on his jacket and left the house. He saw the bus he needed approaching and had to run down the road in order to catch it. When he had met his friend, they went to a bowling alley and played there for several hours. By this time they were ready for lunch so they went to a café for beans on toast. They stayed there for an hour chatting and deciding what to do next and agreed to go to the local cinema to watch an action film.

Variation

Draw a simple cartoon sequence. Show it to the students for a minute, then ask them to write down what was happening in the correct order.

UNDERSTANDING

Understanding is the key to developing a personal response to taught material. It moves beyond familiarity, which can be repetition in its simplest form, to comprehension, whereby students may start to think independently about what has been taught and use their mental processes to synthesise information. Understanding is the first step towards the mastery of higher order thinking skills and is the foundation upon which learning is built.

Why am I ...?

This activity focuses the students' understanding on the reasons for doing something and how these reasons can be linked in to a wider story.

 Group size: Individual

 Time: 20–30 minutes

 Resources: Paper and pencils

What to do

Ask for ten volunteers to perform action mimes. The remaining students must write a sentence after each mime, incorporating it into a storyline to explain the reason for the action. For example:

The first student mimes 'digging'. The story might begin:

- Nathan was digging in his potato patch because he wanted mashed potatoes for tea.

The second student might mime 'swimming' and the story could continue:

- He stepped backwards and accidentally fell into the river, which started to carry him out to sea.

The next student might mime 'writing' and the storyline could say:

- He was able to swim to shore where he found a scrap of paper on the bank and, using a pencil from his pocket, he wrote a note asking for help, before he was carried away again by the current.

When they have finished writing, the students compare their stories.

Variation

To add to the humour, the students could pass on their papers each time, as in the game 'Consequences', so that each new sentence is completed by a different student.

Whodunnit? You decide

This activity helps the students to develop an understanding of motives and a chain of events.

Group size: 8

Time: 30+ minutes

Resources: None

What to do

Put the students in groups of eight. One student is the chairperson and the remaining seven are each given a different character. The chairperson reads the statement:

'Lord Pickles was found dead in his stables this morning. He had been hit on the head with a horse shoe.'

The list of characters are: Lady Pickles (his wife), Rupert Pickles (his son), Jeeves the butler, Henry the stable boy, Elizabeth the maid, Mr/s Taylor the racehorse trainer and Sir Peter Barrington (his business partner). Each student has to present a motive to explain the murder, the more complicated the better. They can also implicate other characters in their story. The chairperson decides whose story is best and therefore who the murderer is.

Extension

Ask each group to think of a different scenario and group of characters. For example, it could be a burglary, or secret agent assignment. The groups take turns to explain their scenario and group of characters. Each character then provides their motive for the rest of the class to decide 'whodunnit'.

I have sharp teeth because ...

In this activity, students discuss the characteristics of certain animals. They understand the purpose of such characteristics and how these benefit the animal. They are also made aware that they must give detailed explanations in order to deliver information effectively.

Group size: Pairs or groups of 3–4

Time: 20–30 minutes

Resources: Paper and pencils

What to do

Put the students into pairs or small groups. Read the following statements and ask the students to discuss and write down their answers. At the end, let the students compare their answers.

I am a tiger and I have sharp teeth because …

I am a shark and I am white on the bottom and grey on the top because …

I am a gazelle and I have long legs because …

I am a lion and I kill the cubs of other males because …

I am a horse and I have a long mane and tail because …

I am a moth and I am shaped like a leaf because …

I am a hyena and I hunt in a pack because …

I am a zebra and I have stripes because …

I am a cow and I have to eat grass for many hours because …

I am a wildebeest and I live in a herd because …

Extension

Give the students a list of attributes and ask them to draw a corresponding animal. For example, draw a bird that can wade in water, can poke its beak in between rocks, is camouflaged in snow, has unusual chest markings and a long tail to attract females.

Because, because, because

In this activity, students develop their ability to understand statements and are reminded that all statements need to be explained.

 Group size: Individual

 Time: 10–20 minutes

 Resources: None

What to do

The students sit in a circle. Start the activity by making a statement, such as 'The robin in my garden has a red breast because …' The student next to you has to provide an explanation and then end the sentence with 'because'. The following student has to provide additional information also ending with 'because' and so on around the circle. The explanations don't have to be true or valid, but have to build on the previous explanations. For example:

• The robin in my garden has a red breast because …

• Red is his favourite colour because …

• He likes to eat strawberries because …

• He goes to Wimbledon every year to eat strawberries and cream because …

• He likes to watch the tennis because …

• He loves the fluffy, round tennis balls because …

• They remind him of his mother because …

Extension

When you have played this game several times and can get all the way round the circle, play 'Beat the clock' and time the activity. Aim to decrease your time whenever you play.

Follow my instructions

This activity is very useful as a five-minute introduction to the concept of understanding. It demonstrates the importance of providing details when communicating information, in order to be fully understood.

 Group size: Pairs

 Time: 5–15 minutes

 Resources: None

What to do

Put the students into pairs. They take it in turns to give instructions to their partner on how to perform a simple task. The partner can only do exactly what they are told. They can't fill in missing instructions from their own knowledge and experience. So, if the instruction was to clean teeth, the student would have to give specific details of every step: pick up the toothpaste and unscrew the cap, pick up the toothbrush, put toothpaste on the toothbrush, turn on the water, put the toothbrush in the mouth and brush the teeth, rinse the toothbrush under the tap and brush teeth again. You can give the students suggestions for suitable tasks such as making a cup of tea, putting a letter in an envelope, making a sandwich. Warn them not to choose overly difficult or complicated tasks at first.

Extension

Ask for volunteer pairs to demonstrate their instructions and mimes and encourage the other students to check if the instructions are specific enough. Tell them to watch out for any actions that the mimer does without being told.

Ickle wuffer

This activity requires the students to demonstrate understanding of context in order to make sense of the sentences.

 Group size: Individual

 Time: 15–20 minutes

 Resources: Whiteboard and pen; paper and pencils

What to do

Put the following lists of adjectives and nouns onto the board:

Tall, strong, thin, happy, fast, heavy, beautiful, loud, smelly, black
Car, man, horse, bridge, house, necklace, ball, book, case, cheese

Think of a sentence containing several of these words, such as 'The thin man was carrying a heavy case'. Write the sentence on the board but substitute the adjectives and nouns for nonsense words, for example 'The ickle wuffer was carrying a drongo boodle'. Explain to the students what you have done and ask them to try and work out the sentence using words from the list to make sense. (If they come up with a sentence that differs from yours, but makes perfect sense, that's fine.) Ask the students to each make up their own sentence in this manner, substituting words from the list with their own nonsense words. They can then try and work out each other's sentences. Tell the students that their sentences must make sense. So, for example, they can't write something like 'The smelly necklace jumped over the black house'.

Extension

With higher attainment groups, you can ask the students to think of their own lists of adjectives and nouns. They could ask other students to have a go at working out their nonsense sentence, before showing them their list of words.

Slang it up

In this activity, students show that they are able to understand the connections between objects and their slang names, and that they can think up slang terms of their own.

Group size: Pairs

Time: 15–20 minutes

Resources: Whiteboard and pen; paper and pencils

What to do

Write the words 'ice', 'bling' and 'rocks' on the board and explain that they are slang terms for diamonds. Put the students into pairs and ask them to discuss why these words have been chosen to represent diamonds. Ask for volunteers to say what conclusions they have reached. With the students remaining in their pairs, split the class in half. Give one half the words: chair, swimming pool, cat, television and camera and the other half the words: radio, cup, baby, skating rink and tree. Ask the students to think up three slang terms for each of their words. The slang terms must have a logical connection to the given word.

Extension

Ask each pair to join up with a pair from the other half. They take turns to say one set of three slang words that they have invented, and the other pair must guess the original word and say how they guessed.

Watch my face

In this activity, students have to recognise facial expressions and show understanding of the associated emotion. They have to think beyond the explicit visual clues to understand reasons and motives.

Group size: 3

Time: 10–15 minutes

Resources: Paper and pencils

What to do

Put the students into groups of three. One student in each group volunteers to make different facial expressions (or if you prefer, they can take turns to do this). The remaining two students confer and write down a brief description of each facial expression and the associated feeling. Ask the students why it is important to be able to read facial expressions and other non-verbal signs. Discuss how this knowledge helps them to form their responses to other people.

Variation

Instead of asking students to mime, you can use photographs of people's expressions showing different emotions from a resources pack, if available, or taken from magazines.

Read all about it

This activity focuses the students' attention on the details of a story and reminds them that statements need to be explained in order to be fully understood.

Group size: 4–6

Time: 30+ minutes

Resources: A selection of magazines and newspapers; for each group, a large sheet of plain paper

What to do

Put the students into mixed ability groups. Ask them to choose a headline from the following list and make up a story using words or sentences cut from the magazines and newspapers. The sentences must make sense and follow on logically.

1. Thirteen-year-old boy wins Olympic Gold.

2. Queen to star in *Eastenders* as landlady of the Queen Vic.

3. Alien spaceship lands in Wiltshire field.

4. Scientists breed six-legged horse.

5. Divers discover golden city beneath the sea.

Variation

Give a different headline to each group. The students are allowed ten minutes in which to create one paragraph and then the sheets are moved on to the next group. Allow sufficient time for each group to add to every story.

Superhero/supervillain

This activity demonstrates that while students can make an initial judgement, further study will produce a deeper understanding.

Group size: Individual

Time: 30+ minutes

Resources: Paper and coloured pencils/felt-tips; a selection of photographs of superheroes or villains such as Spiderman, Batman, Iceman, Iron Man, The Penguin, The Joker, The Green Goblin and Dr Octopus

What to do

Show the students the images you have collected of the superheroes or villains. Explain that the students could guess the characters' individual powers by looking at their appearance, and that their powers are connected to their names. Discuss these with the students for each image. For example, Spiderman can climb up walls and make webs in which to trap villains. Ask the students to create a picture of their own superhero/villain. The name must reflect the character's appearance and also be connected to the powers that they possess.

Extension

The students look at each other's drawings to guess the name of the superhero/villain and state what they think the character's powers are. They must explain why they have given these answers.

How they relate

This activity encourages students to consider the importance of description and explanation in developing understanding.

Group size: Pairs or groups of 3–4

Time: 15–30 minutes

Resources: Paper and pencils; a selection of random objects such as a necklace, shell, key, flower, wallet, hat

What to do

Put the students into pairs or small groups. Give each group two items from the selection of random objects. Depending on the level of attainment in your class, ask the groups to write a paragraph or short story that incorporates both objects. Their text must make sense. The groups can take turns to show the rest of the class their objects and read their texts.

Variation

Give each group the same two objects to see how similar/different their storylines are.

And then what happens?

This activity demonstrates the importance of clear explanations and logical sequencing to assist understanding.

 Group size: 3–4

 Time: 30+ minutes

 Resources: Paper and pencils, scissors, glue sticks

What to do

Put the students into small groups and ask them to write a narrative in 20 lines (you can vary the number of lines according to the attainment level of your class), with the action following on sequentially. They then cut the text into 20 separate lines and jumble them up. The groups swap their texts and try to assemble the narrative into the correct order. Discuss with the students what helped or hindered them in completing this task.

Variation

Choose a factual description of a task from a suitable textbook, such as a recipe book, and give pairs of students a jumbled version to put into the correct order.

Acting out

This activity encourages students to use their understanding in order to make connections.

 Group size: Divide class into two equal groups

 Time: 20–30 minutes

 Resources: Two copies of the photocopiable sheet *Headlines* (p. 128).

What to do

Cut one of the photocopied sheets into individual headlines and fold so that the writing cannot be seen by the students. Divide the class into two groups and give each group half of the folded headlines. The students take turns to take a headline and mime the action for the others in their group to guess. For lower attainment groups, you can display the list or read all the headlines before they begin the activity.

Extension

Ask the students to think of their own set of bizarre headlines and repeat the activity.

Walk this way

In this activity the students demonstrate their understanding of how emotions affect expressions and body language.

 Group size: Individual

 Time: 15–20 minutes

 Resources: Whiteboard and pen

What to do

Ask the students to call out the names of different emotions, such as anger, fear, joy, excitement, loneliness, sadness, anxiety, and list them on the board. Ask for a volunteer to choose one of the emotions from the board and to walk in front of the other students with an appropriate expression and in a manner that displays the chosen emotion. They must not say the emotion out loud. The watching students try to guess the correct emotion. Cross that emotion off the list and ask for another volunteer to choose a different emotion to display.

Extension

Just for fun, ask the students to make up different walks for when it is sunny, raining, freezing, windy, stormy and foggy. Let volunteers perform their walks and explain why they have chosen those particular movements.

INSIGHT

Insight moves beyond mere understanding as students begin to use their own intuitive perception and prior knowledge to comprehend the true nature of what is taught. Awareness of their own ability to offer insightful opinions can bolster a student's confidence in responding independently to stimulus material, as they are able to make connections between personal knowledge and what is taught. This will help to increase the value of the fundamental concepts and knowledge they are taught in the classroom. Their own insight forges links between this, which can be seen as purely academic, and what they know of the 'real world'.

Mop it up

In this activity, the students use their knowledge and understanding in an insightful way to produce an imaginary machine.

 Group size: Pairs

 Time: 15–20 minutes

 Resources: Paper and pencils

What to do

Put the students into pairs. Explain that they are going to design an imaginary machine that will carry out a chore for them, such as mopping the floor, making a cup of tea, walking the dog, or feeding the baby. They must think of all the stages involved in the chore and make sure that they include all the necessary parts in their machine. The students then show their design to other pairs to see if they can guess the task involved.

Extension

Ask the students to choose a task and challenge other pairs to design a machine that will fulfil their task. You could put all the tasks into a box and ask each pair to pick one out unseen. The students could then try and guess whose task they had picked.

Age appropriate

The students use their insight to evaluate the needs, likes and dislikes of less familiar age brackets.

 Group size: Individual

 Time: 15–20 minutes

 Resources: Paper and pencils

What to do

Explain to the pupils that they are going to design a cartoon character who would appeal to people of a certain age bracket. They are not allowed to choose their own age group, so must rely on their knowledge and understanding of other ages. They might, for example, choose toddlers, children, adults aged 30–40 years or the elderly. They must explain why they think their design would appeal to the age bracket that they have chosen. In other words, they must consider the attributes of that particular age group.

Variation

To add a further dimension to the activity, you could tell the students that their cartoon character must be designed for the opposite gender.

Radio show

The students demonstrate their insight into media requirements by devising a radio show for their peers.

 Group size: 3–4

 Time: 40+ minutes

 Resources: Paper and pencils

What to do

Put the students into small groups. Explain that they are going to devise a radio programme that they think would appeal to people of their own age. They need to consider what topics of conversation could be included, choose two celebrities to appear on the show, select three songs that would be played, design a competition that would appeal to the listeners (stating the prize involved) and incorporate an advertisement break with three or four advertisements. When they have completed this, ask each group to describe their radio show to the other students. You could take the best from each group and record a show that the students could play to other classes.

Extension

Ask each group to devise another radio show, incorporating all the same features, but for a different age bracket.

Who's it for?

The students use their insight to decide which target audience a selection of advertisements would appeal to.

Group size: Pairs

Time: 20–30 minutes

Resources: Paper and pencils; a selection of 20–30 advertisements from different magazines, designed to appeal to different age ranges

What to do

Number each advertisement and display them for the students to see. Put the students into pairs and explain that they are going to discuss with their partner which age range they think each advertisement was designed for. They write down all the numbers and an appropriate age beside them. When they have completed this task, arrange the advertisements into age-related categories with them. Discuss what clues helped them to make their decisions. Were there any advertisements that they thought had universal appeal or might belong to more than one category?

Variation

Display a selection of gender-related advertisements and ask the students to decide which gender each is intended for. Try to include some that might appeal to both genders.

In the style of …

The students use their insight to develop scenes in a variety of different genres.

 Group size: 5–6

 Time: 40+ minutes

 Resources: None

What to do

Explain to the students that they will be put into groups and are then going to make up a short scene for a film. Each group will choose a different genre for their scene and all groups will begin from the same starting point. You can ask the students to suggest different genres such as musical, horror, western, romantic comedy, science fiction, thriller and soap opera. Put the students into groups of five or six and ensure that each group has a different genre. Their starting point is that one character walks into a room and asks, 'Where's Joe?' and a second character responds with, 'Why?' Allow time for the groups to develop their scenes and then call the students together to perform for one another.

Variation

Instead of allowing the students to choose, give each group a different genre, telling them not to say this aloud. They devise and perform their scenes to one another and the students have to guess the genre for each group.

Where do we belong?

This activity encourages the students to develop critical insight as they try to work out the relevant categories to which their words belong.

Group size: Individual

Time: 10–15 minutes

Resources: One copy of the photocopiable sheet *Where do we belong?* (p. 129).

What to do

Cut out the words from the sheet and give them out to the students. For low attainment groups you can display the category words, and give out the more unfamiliar words to the higher attaining students. For higher attainment groups, distribute the words randomly among the class and let the students decide what the categories are. Try and use an even number from each category. There are sufficient words for a class of 30 students. With fewer students you can either select four or five words from each category or leave a category out. Explain that the words relate to different places they might be. You could give examples such as 'library' and 'train'. There will probably be some unfamiliar words. They must try and group themselves (sitting or standing) according to the relevant category. This is a whole class activity and the students must help one another. If you want to, you can tell the students how many words are in each category.

Extension

With the students' help, write some new category headings onto slips of paper. Put these into a container. Put the students into five groups and ask each group to pick out a new heading. They think of four to six words (depending on the number in the class) relating to their heading and write them onto slips of paper. The slips of paper are distributed randomly and the activity is repeated.

Speak out

In this activity, the students use their insight into human nature to develop their fictional characters.

 Group size: 5–6

 Time: 20–30 minutes

 Resources: A list of characters: a boy, a girl, two friends of each, a parent of the boy and girl, a policeman, a local person living in the same neighbourhood

What to do

Put the students into groups and give them one or more of the characters. Describe a scenario that is loosely based on the story of Romeo and Juliet. The boy and girl are sweethearts from warring families. The local person is not involved with either family. The characters are going to take part in a chat show, each giving their side of the story and what they think should happen. The groups discuss what their characters might say and how they might behave and choose someone to play each role. The characters are brought out one at a time to have their say and to be questioned by the chat show host. This can be the teacher or a student.

Extension

The students who are not involved in the role play can become the audience and ask questions relating to the background, lives and involvement in the plot of any of the characters.

Design a ride

This activity encourages the students to use their insight into what thrills and excites people, by designing a ride for an adventure park.

Group size: Pairs or groups of 3–4

Time: 15–20 minutes

Resources: Paper and pencils

What to do

Discuss the rides at theme and adventure parks with the students, giving consideration to what makes a thrilling ride. Put the students into pairs or small groups and ask them to design a new ride. They can base it on a theme if they like. For example, there are rides in Disney theme parks based on films or books such as *Jaws*. The groups can either describe or draw and label their ride. When all the groups have finished, they can take turns to present their ride to the other students.

Extension

Talk with the students about a real-life thrill they might like to experience, such as sky-diving, pot-holing or crocodile wrestling.

Who, what, where, when and why?

Students use their insight to interpret the events shown in a photograph.

 Group size: Pairs or groups of 3–4

 Time: 20–30 minutes

 Resources: Choose a photograph from a magazine, or print one from an internet news source, that shows something happening: for example, a man shouting in the street, or a group of people watching something

What to do

Put the students into pairs or small groups and display the photograph. Ask the students to study the photograph then discuss in their groups their thoughts on the following. Who is/are the person/people involved in the photograph? What is happening? Where is it happening? When is it happening and why is it happening? They can write down their decisions. Ask each group, in turn, to explain their thoughts on the photograph.

Extension

Ask the students to return to their groups and decide what they think happened next.

Talent show

This activity encourages the students to use their insight into what would constitute a successful act for a talent show.

 Group size: Individual

 Time: 10–15 minutes

 Resources: Paper and pencils

What to do

Explain to the students that they are going to think of an act they believe would win a talent show contest. This act could involve singing, dancing, acrobatics, animals or various props. They must give explanations of why they consider their act to be a potential winner. What are the features that make it especially good?

Extension

Discuss with the students the definition of talent. Do they think everyone has a talent? Do they think that views of what constitutes a talent may vary from country to country? If so, would this make them revise their definition?

Going round

In this activity, students use insight into professions and situations to work out probable pairings.

 Group size: Divide the class into two equal groups

 Time: 20–30 minutes

 Resources: One copy of the photocopiable sheet *Going round* (pp. 130–131)

What to do

Photocopy and cut out the questions and answers (do not include the names/job titles of the speakers). Explain to the class that you have a set of questions and answers that go together and give some examples. Divide the class into two equal groups. Give out the questions to one half and the answers to the other half. Tell the students to look at their slips of paper, but they must not say out loud what is written. The groups form two circles one inside the other, with the outside group being the question askers and facing inwards. The inner circle is formed by the students with the answers, and they face outwards. Each student from the inner circle faces a student in the outer circle. The activity commences with all the students in the outside circle asking their questions. The students facing them give their answers. If the students think their question and answers match they leave the circle and sit in their pairs. If they don't match, on your command, the inside circle moves one place in an anti-clockwise direction. The activity continues like this until all the students are correctly paired.

Variation

Hand out the slips of paper randomly. Ask the class to mill around, repeating their question and answer repeatedly. They must also listen carefully to try and find their matching question or answer.

Fire burn and cauldron bubble

This activity requires the students to use their insight into how to create a spooky atmosphere using modern language.

 Group size: Pairs or groups of 3–4

 Time: 20–30 minutes

 Resources: For each pair or group, a copy of photocopiable sheet *Fire burn and cauldron bubble* (pp. 132–133), which contains the three witches' charm from the beginning of Act IV, Scene 1 of *Macbeth* by William Shakespeare

What to do

Put the class into pairs or small groups, each with a copy of the witches' charm. Read through the scene with the students, discussing the language used and how it evokes a spooky atmosphere. Ask the students to write a modern version of a charm, which sets a similar scene. They can do this in the form of a rap if they so choose. When the students have completed this activity, they can take turns to read out their charms in appropriate witch-like voices.

Variation

Turn the activity into a game in which the students sit in a circle and take turns to think of different ingredients for a charm. If they can't think of a charm or repeat an earlier one, they are out.

Constellations

This activity encourages the students to use insight along with comprehension as they try to work out star constellations.

 Group size: Pairs

 Time: 20–30 minutes

 Resources: Paper and pencils; illustrations of various star constellations

What to do

Show the students the illustrations of star constellations. Discuss with them how the figures are represented by stars at a few key points, but the whole outline is not there. Put the students into pairs and ask them to work out a constellation for a figure they invent, such as a hunter or an animal. When they have done this, ask for a volunteer to tell the class what figure they have chosen. Instruct the other students to try and draw the star constellation that might represent this figure. Compare their attempts with the original pair's drawing and see whose is the closest. Repeat with other constellations.

Variation

Ask the pairs to draw a random arrangement of stars. They swap with another pair and think of a figure that could fit into a constellation within the random arrangement.

A Wadjiko

The students use insight to think of the attributes a carnivore might have, and draw and label an animal with those attributes.

Group size: Pairs

Time: 15–20 minutes

Resources: Paper and pencils

What to do

Put the students into pairs. Explain that they are going to make up an animal called a Wadjiko. It is a carnivore and lives in Africa. They must draw the animal and label the attributes that would make it a successful carnivore. They can discuss these with their partner. When the students have finished, ask for volunteers to show their drawings and describe the attributes they have given their animal.

Extension

Ask the students to think of an animal attribute that would be useful for the following purposes: camouflage, defence, to reach leaves at the top of trees, to live underground, to run quickly, to attract a mate.

Websites

The students must use the insight they have gained from visiting social network websites to create a new site.

Group size: 4–6

Time: 20–30 minutes

Resources: Paper and pencils

What to do

Put the students into groups. Explain that they are going to design a new social network website, like Facebook or Twitter, for their age group. Within their groups, they must discuss the attributes that make a website successful and apply these to their design. Encourage the students to thoroughly discuss and consider what teenagers want from these sites.

Extension

Ask each group to present their new site to the class and take a vote to discover the most popular. Groups cannot vote for their own site.

ANALYSIS

Analysis is the ability to examine material carefully and separate it into its constituent parts or elements, while at the same time making personal judgements regarding the findings. Analysis focuses students on stimulus material and aids concentration. It is an important and valuable cross-curricular skill.

What's my line?

The students must analyse the text in order to work out the professions of various people.

Group size: Individual

Time: 10–15 minutes

Resources: The texts below can either be read to the students or copied for them from photocopiable sheet *What's my line?* (p. 134)

What to do

Read out or hand out the texts below and ask the students to try and guess the professions involved. They must list the words or phrases that help them to make their decisions.

1.

'Another busy day ahead. I've several visits to make before I get to base. Old Mrs Morris tells me about her granddaughter's wedding as I hold her hand. She's looking remarkably well for 85. Mrs Patel tells me all about her baby's red rash and how he's very fretful – I expect he's just teething, but I take his temperature anyway. Back at base, a dozen hopeful faces look at me as I walk through to my room. Someone has a very nasty cough – sounds like bronchitis – I'll have to prescribe antibiotics. I hope everyone else doesn't catch it.'

2.

'I drive past the park for the fifth time that day. I wish I was out there sitting in the cool shade of a tree. The sun beats down through the large windscreen and I am so hot. I stop at the church, passengers get on, then I'm off again. Traffic's bad today. There's roadworks on my route and my vehicle is large and not easy to turn. Behind me, people sit in pairs and chatter or listen to music on their headphones.'

3.

'I'm hoping the rain holds off long enough to do the mowing. The roses are covered in greenfly – a wash with a weak soapy solution, I think, will cure that. I prop the spade against the wall. The hole's big enough for the root ball of this sapling. Looks like there'll be a good crop of redcurrants this year.'

Professions

1. Doctor

2. Bus driver

3. Gardener

Extension

Put the students into pairs and ask them to make up a similar text about a different profession. Put all the texts into a box and pull them out, one at a time, to read to the class for them to guess the profession. Students must not 'guess' their own text.

Watch my actions carefully

The students must analyse the mimed actions in order to work out what is being related.

 Group size: Individual

 Time: 15+ minutes

 Resources: One copy of the photocopiable sheet *Mimes* (p. 135)

What to do

Photocopy the list of mimes and cut out each one separately. Fold and put the mimes into a container. Ask for volunteers to take a statement from the box and mime an appropriate action. The other students must try and guess what they are doing.

Variation

If you think that your students will find this activity difficult, you can display the list of mimes for them to see.

Disney film tableau

The students must analyse the positions of the figures in a tableau to try and work out the Disney film that it depicts.

Group size: 5–6

Time: 20–30 minutes

Resources: A list of Disney films compiled by the students

What to do

With the students, compile a list of Disney films. Cut the list into individual film titles and place in a container. Put the students into groups of five or six and let each group take a film name from the container. Spread the groups out, so that they don't overhear one another, and ask them to devise a tableau that depicts a famous scene from their film. Invite each group, in turn, to show their tableau and ask the other students to guess the film.

Variation

You could use nursery rhymes or fairy stories as the subject, but compile the list with the students to make sure that they know the chosen titles.

Native American names

The students analyse Native American names and discuss possible reasons why the names were given.

Group size: 3–4

Time: 15–20 minutes

Resources: Paper and pencils

What to do

Native American names were influenced by religion, nature and desired personality traits. Choose a few names from the list below and discuss their possible meanings with the students. For example, 'Sight of Day' might mean someone born at dawn and 'Sturdy Oak' might mean a big male. Put the students into groups of three or four and ask them to analyse and write down the possible meanings of the names in the list. When they have done this, call the students together to compare their reasons.

Sight of Day	Stays at Home
Yellow Leaf	Butterfly
Turtle	Time of Waiting Moon
Little Wolf	Red Cloud
Sturdy Oak	Flute Girl
Rippling Brook	Keeper of the Flame
One who Lives Below	Hole in the Sky
Many Coyotes	Hanging over the Top

Extension

Ask the students to come up with a Native American-type name that they think describes them. It can be either a single word or a phrase.

Quick thinking

Students use their analytical skills against the clock in this activity designed to encourage the use of scanning.

Group size: Individual or pairs

Time: 20 minutes

Resources: For each student or pair of students, a copy of the photocopiable sheet *Quick thinking* (p. 136)

What to do

The students can work individually or, if you think they might find this activity quite difficult, in pairs. Hand out the photocopied sheets. Read through the text, while the students follow. Explain that they will have five to ten minutes, depending on the attainment level of your students, in which to complete as many questions as possible.

At the end of the allotted time, go through the questions and see who has completed the most.

Answers to the questions

1. They had included Brad Loxley and his ...

2. Nine

3. Clutterbucks

4. Twelve

5. Four

6. Clumber, Clutterbucks, Didgery, Handlebar, Loxley, Nosebag, Slipperyeel, Sonar, Stinkhorn

7. Dr Handlebar

8. Fourteen

9. Fewer

10. Prototype.

Variation

For high attaining students, you could ask them to complete all the questions in the shortest time possible.

Making sense

Students must analyse a piece of text in which all the spaces between words have been removed, in order to make sense of it.

 Group size: Individual

 Time: 15–20 minutes

 Resources: For each student, a copy of the photocopiable sheet *Making sense* (p. 137)

What to do

Hand out the photocopied text to the students and explain that all the spaces between the words have been removed. They must try to work out where the spaces were and make sense of the text in order to answer the questions beneath.

Extension

Ask the students to make up a paragraph or select one from a book and remove the spaces. They must think of a suitable question to accompany their text. The students swap and analyse each other's texts.

Put together

The students must analyse shapes on a piece of paper to work out a jigsaw puzzle of patterns.

Group size: 6–8

Time: 15–20 minutes

Resources: The photocopiable sheet *Put together* (p. 138) copied onto an A3 sheet of paper to enlarge the patterns

What to do

Decide how many students will be in each group, ideally six to eight, and cut as many jigsaw pieces from the patterns as required. If the number of students can't be divided into equal groups, you can cut the patterns accordingly so that some have more component parts than others. Hand out the puzzle pieces randomly, one to each student. They must study their sections and find other students with corresponding parts before putting the pieces of the five puzzles together. For lower attaining groups, they could all be given the same jigsaw, but use all five puzzles with higher attaining groups.

Extension

Try a whole class exercise by cutting a picture into as many parts as there are students. Hand the pieces out randomly and ask the students to work together to make up the picture.

Zoom in

The students use their analytical skills to try and work out the identity of an object from one small section of a photograph that is displayed.

Group size: Individual

Time: 15–20 minutes

Resources: A selection of photographs of everyday objects, such as a vacuum cleaner, a kettle, a bicycle, a razor, a table lamp, a computer keyboard. Alternatively, you can use computer-generated photographs and zoom in on one small section.

What to do

Cover up most of each photograph, leaving one small section visible. Show each photograph in turn and ask the students if they can guess what the object is by studying the small part that is visible. If they find any of the photographs difficult to guess, you could uncover the object gradually to see when they can give the correct answer.

Variation

Create silhouettes of everyday objects, by drawing round illustrations onto black paper and cutting out the shapes. See if the students can guess their identity.

How many?

Students analyse a busy picture in order to answer questions.

Group size: Pairs

Time: 10–20 minutes

Resources: For each pair of students, a copy of the two photocopiable sheets *How many?*, the picture and the questions (pp. 139–140)

What to do

Put the students into pairs and give each pair a copy of the picture and the questions. Give them a set time (10 to 20 minutes), depending on the attainment level of the students, to answer as many questions as possible.

Answers

1. A violin.
2. Five.
3. Four.
4. A bunch of flowers.
5. A bottle.
6. A hat with a large brim and a flower.
7. Twenty-one.
8. Eggs.
9. A pigeon.
10. Five.
11. A diamond.
12. A short-sleeved top.
13. Twelve.
14. Under the bench by the bag shop.
15. Eight.
16. Balloons.
17. A suitcase and a walking stick.
18. A little girl.
19. The bag shop.
20. Luigi's restaurant.
    Pizza – buy one get one free!

Extension

Tell the students to turn over their pictures and answer the following questions from memory. Answers can be given either verbally or in writing.

1. Why is a dog running through the mall?

2. What is the food stall downstairs selling?

3. What unusual bird could you see?

4. What has the baby thrown out of the push chair?

5. What is falling out of an old lady's shopping trolley?

6. The person with the walking stick is in front of which shop?

Answers

1. It is chasing a cat.

2. Doughnuts.

3. A penguin.

4. A bottle.

5. Some carrots.

6. The bookshop.

Which line is longer?

The students must analyse a set of drawings to work out how optical illusions have been created.

Group size: Pairs

Time: 15–20 minutes

Resources: For each pair of students, a copy of the photocopiable sheets *Which line is longer?* (pp. 141–142) and, for the Extension activity, sheet *What do you see?* (p. 143)

What to do

Put the students into pairs and give each pair a copy of the photocopied sheets. Ask them to complete the questions on the sheets. Go through the items and explain that they are optical illusions and the lines and circles are, in fact, the same size in each image. Ask the students how the illusions are created in each item.

Extension

Show the students the illustration of the vase/faces (photocopiable sheet *What do you see?*, p. 143) and ask them what they can see. How many people first saw the vase? The faces? This is based on the famous Rubin's vase image, devised in the early 20th century by the Danish psychologist Edgar Rubin.

Shoe prints

The students must analyse the size, shape and distinguishing marks on each shoe print to decide who it belongs to.

Group size: 3–4

Time: 20–30 minutes

Resources: Make prints of each student's right shoe. You can either do this with a dusty print on white paper or put chalk over the sole and print onto black paper

What to do

Put the students into small groups with a selection of shoe prints. They must look at the size, shape and distinguishing marks and try and work out whose shoe the print belongs to. Call the students together and let each group in turn check to see if their guesses are correct.

Extension

If your school has a sand pit, you could try the following activity. Ask all the students to face away from the sand. Ask for a volunteer to choose a method of moving, for example running, skipping, walking backwards, hopping, jumping through the sand. The other students turn round and by analysing the marks in the sand, try to work out the method of movement. Rake the sand smooth and repeat with another volunteer.

INTERPRETATION

Interpretation involves the ability to give a personal view of stimulus material. In explaining their own interpretation, students can offer alternative ideas and responses and, as such, gain confidence in their ownership of personal opinions that may differ from an author, a theory or other students. Interpretation is a very valuable skill to master in developing true independent thinking, as students can then use the curriculum as a springboard to explore different aspects of the offered material rather than thinking that the subject consists of only what is taught in their lessons.

Interpret the letter

The students are required to interpret visual clues to decipher a letter.

Group size: Individual or pairs

Time: 15–20 minutes

Resources: Paper and pencils; for each student or pair of students, a copy of the photocopiable sheet *Interpret the letter* (p. 144)

What to do

The students can work individually or in pairs to read the letter. Hand out the copied letter and explain that it has been written in drawings rather than words. Tell the students that some of the clues are based on phonetics rather than the correct spelling of a word, such as 'm(eye)' for 'my'. If the students have difficulty interpreting one of the drawings, tell them to find the words surrounding it and try to guess the missing word from its context.

Extension

Depending on their level of attainment, ask the students to write a sentence/paragraph using drawings.

Designing sets

The students are asked to interpret a list of instructions in order to design a stage set.

Group size: Individual

Time: 20–30 minutes

Resources: Paper and pencils

What to do

Explain to the students that you are going to read the design instructions for a stage set for an imaginary play. They can make notes while you read and, afterwards, they must draw a design for the set, based on the information you have given them. Encourage the students to add details such as colours and textures where appropriate. Read out the text below.

'This set is very atmospheric and magical, but in a rather creepy, scary way. There are two doors, both different and with unusual features. A strange table is at centre stage, above which hangs a light in the shape of an animal's head. A large, gloomy picture takes up most of one wall. The overall impression is dark and dismal.'

Variation

If you have the time, you could ask the students to work in pairs or small groups to make a set within a cardboard box that represents the stage.

Hand gestures

The students have to interpret hand gestures to guess their meaning.

 Group size: Pairs or groups of 3–4

 Time: 15–20 minutes

 Resources: None

What to do

Explain to the students that we often use hand gestures to convey meaning. Give them a few examples, such as waving hello and goodbye, beckoning and conveying 'I'm watching you' by pointing to self, using the index finger and middle finger of one hand to point to your eyes and then pointing to a student. The students will probably be familiar with these gestures. Make up several more for them to guess. For example, point to someone and mime holding a cup and drinking to enquire 'Would you like a drink?' Point to someone and yawn to enquire 'Are you tired?' Perhaps you could gesture instructions to leave the classroom and take a message somewhere or give someone a computer task. Put the students into pairs or small groups and ask them to make up some gestures for the others to guess.

Extension

Ask the students if they can use other body gestures to convey meaning. They are not allowed to use hands expressively.

The Mullet

The students are asked to interpret words in relation to hairstyles, then make some up themselves.

Group size: Pairs or groups of 3–4

Time: 20 minutes

Resources: Paper and pencils

What to do

Discuss with the students the term 'Mullet' in relation to a particular hairstyle. Ask them how they think the name of a fish came to be associated with a hairstyle. Put the students into groups or pairs. Ask them to draw or describe in words the hairstyle they imagine would be associated with the following terms: Catherine wheel, flip-flop, Cornish pasty. Ask the students to think of two new terms to describe particular hairstyles and then to ask other students to guess what their terms describe.

Extension

Talk to the students about clothes that certain groups might wear, for example punks, Goths, Romantics. Can they think up some new styles and terms to describe them?

Paint splodge

The students give their interpretations of a paint splodge then create more for others to interpret.

 Group size: Individual

 Time: 15–20 minutes

 Resources: Paper and paint; one copy of the photocopiable sheet *Paint splodge* (p. 145) copied large enough for the whole class to see

What to do

Display the paint splodge to the students. Ask them what they think it represents. In other words, what does it make them think of? Encourage them to give their immediate reactions. Ask the students to tell you their reactions and discuss the variety of responses that you get. Why do they think that people have different perceptions of the splodge? Ask the students to create a paint splodge and show it to other students. How varied are the responses that they get?

This activity is inspired by the well-known inkblot tests devised by Hermann Rorschach.

Extension

Play a tape of short music excerpts and ask the students what mood or emotion they would associate with each piece.

What on earth is happening?

The students give imaginative interpretations of described situations.

Group size: Individual, pairs or groups of 3–4

Time: 20–30 minutes

Resources: Paper and pencils

What to do

The students can work individually, in pairs or small groups for this activity. Display the text describing the three situations below. Ask the students to make up a scenario that interprets the actions and then to say what happens next. Encourage them to use their imaginations and not necessarily to choose what seems to be the most obvious interpretation.

1. Four people are seated in a room. Someone walks into the room, places a parcel on a table and walks out again without speaking or being spoken to by the other people present.

2. Three people are running down a street. They are being chased by someone who is shouting something.

3. Someone is hiding behind a curtain in a room.

Ask for volunteers to read their interpretations and compare the explanations.

Extension

Ask the students to think of a situation. Choose several to read out and ask for verbal interpretations.

What am I playing?

The students interpret drawings of posed figures to make a guess at what the figure is doing.

 Group size: Pairs

 Time: 20–30 minutes

 Resources: A roll of wallpaper, pencils

What to do

Put the students into pairs. Explain that one of the pair is going to pretend that they are a musician. They are going to lie down on a length of wallpaper in a pose, pretending to play an instrument. Their partner is going to draw around them. The pairs take turns to display their drawings and invite the other students to guess what kind of musician they are.

Variation

The students take up the pose of someone playing a sport, for their partner to draw around.

Metaphors

The students give their interpretations of metaphors and then think up some of their own.

 Group size: Pairs or small groups

 Time: 15–20 minutes

 Resources: Paper and pencils

What to do

Put the students into pairs or small groups. Explain to them that a metaphor is a figurative use of a term that is not literally applicable in the given context. For example:

> 'The temperature dropped, the wind rose and I felt a chill enter the air. I looked up at the grey clouds. Above the trees **a black panther snarled, ready to leap forward and devour the sky.**'

In this context, the panther stands for storm clouds.

> 'When she entered the room **a grey fog descended and wrapped us all in its gloomy embrace.**'

Ask the students what this might mean. Perhaps a bad-tempered parent comes into a room of laughing children or someone very sad comes into a room full of happy people.

Ask the students to give their interpretations of the following metaphors.

1. When she opened her mouth a silvery waterfall cascaded over our heads.

2. As he turned from the brightly lit street, a massive ogre lurked at the bottom of the alleyway.

3. The wind whipped the leaves and white rabbits leapt across the sky.

4. The door to our classroom opened and a raging bull entered snorting, with eyes flashing.

Extension

Ask the students to have a go at making up a metaphor of their own. If you think they might find this difficult, you can give them specific situations, for example a metaphor for a large, dark mountain, a snowy field, a shy, timid person.

Fortune cards

The students interpret symbols to explain their likely meanings. They then devise some of their own.

Group size: Individual or pairs

Time: 15–20 minutes

Resources: Paper and pencils; for each student/pair, one copy of photocopiable sheet *Fortune cards* (p. 146)

What to do

The students can do this activity either individually or in pairs. Talk to the students about Tarot cards and how they are used to tell people's fortune. Explain that they are to imagine that the photocopied symbols on the sheet are fortune cards and they must give each card a meaning. Give an example, such as the heart could represent love. When the students have completed the activity, let them compare their interpretations to see how similar/different they are.

Extension

Ask the students to think of two events in life and represent them with a symbol on a fortune card. They show their cards to the other students and invite them to guess their meaning.

Dreams

The students give their interpretations of dreams, then make up dream scenarios for others to interpret.

 Group size: Individual

 Time: 15–20 minutes

 Resources: Paper and pencils

What to do

Talk to the students about the meaning of dreams. Below are some suggested interpretations.

Dream symbols:
airport = a desire for freedom
alley = limited choices
alligator = treachery
ankle = seeking support
ape = deception
arm = nurturing aspect or struggles and challenges in life
bacon = the essentials in life
beach = future is calm and tranquil
birthday cake = best wishes will happen
black = unknown and mysterious
blue = truth and wisdom
cabbage = warning of poverty
cat = creativity and power
cemetery = sadness
chocolate = love and celebration
donkey = lack of understanding
gold = spiritual reward

Chase dreams and falling dreams reflect anxiety.

Read the following dream scenarios and ask the students to give their interpretations of the meanings.

> You walk into a white room. Everyone is wearing white. You say hello to people who are your friends and they don't know you. You try to leave the house but you can't find the way out.

> You are in a dark forest. A black cat walks across your path. You see a bright light in front of you and walk towards it. A smiling man welcomes you into a warm, cosy room.

Extension

Ask for volunteers to describe a vivid dream that they have had and discuss its meaning with the class.

Silent movie sequences

The students are asked to interpret a scenario enacted in silent movie style.

 Group size: 4

 Time: 30+ minutes

 Resources: One copy of the photocopiable sheet *Silent movie sequences* (p. 147)

What to do

Cut up the sheet into separate movie sequences. Put the students into groups of four and give each group one of the movie scenes. Explain that they are going to act out their scene in the style of a silent movie. They are not allowed to speak and must convey emotions through facial gestures and body language. Each group acts out their scene in front of the others. The watching students must interpret the actions to guess what is happening.

Extension

Ask the students to write a series of placards to hold up in front of their scene, as in the silent movie era, to explain the action as it happens.

What's the book?

The students must interpret the texts to decide what type of book each excerpt might be taken from.

Group size: Individual or pairs

Time: 20–30 minutes

Resources: For each student or pair of students, a copy of the photocopiable sheet *What's the book?* (p. 148)

What to do

The students can either work individually or in pairs. Explain to the students that each text represents an excerpt from a different book. They are to read the texts and decide what type of book the excerpt is taken from. If you think they might need some guidance in this, you can talk beforehand about different types of book, such as cookery, fairy stories, travel, detective, poetry.

Answers

1. Detective

2. Travel

3. Cookery

4. Dog training manual

5. Fairy story

6. Poetry

7. Historical

8. Wild flower guide.

Extension

Ask the students to make up a short text that could be an excerpt from a particular type of book and reflects its genre. They swap texts and try to guess what type of book was intended.

Letters from?

The students look at a selection of letters to interpret the text and decide who the letter could be from and to whom it is addressed.

 Group size: Individual or pairs

 Time: 15–20 minutes

 Resources: For each student or pair of students, a copy of the photocopiable sheets *Letters from?* (pp. 149–150)

What to do

The students can work individually or in pairs. Give each student/pair a copy of the letters sheets. Ask them to look at each letter and decide who it could be from and to whom it might be written. Also, what is each letter about? Below are a set of possible answers, but the students may have different ideas.

Answers

1. From a doctor to a patient describing an illness.

2. From a child to an Aunt thanking her for a present.

3. From one friend to another about going to a concert.

4. From a teacher to a pupil about handing in homework.

5. From an adult to a friend or relative while on holiday.

6. From a patient in hospital to a friend describing treatment and recovery.

7. From one friend to another describing a murder mystery weekend.

8. From a charitable organisation to a donor thanking them for supporting their cause.

Extension

Ask the students to think of an animal. They must write a letter from the animal to a friend, describing something about their life. The letter must include clues to their identity. The students read out their letters and invite the others to guess what animal they are.

Check out the scene

The students look at a series of drawings and interpret the visual clues to decide what is happening in each picture.

 Group size: Individual or pairs

 Time: 15–20 minutes

 Resources: For each student or pair of students, a copy of the photocopiable sheet *Check out the scene* (p. 151)

What to do

The students can complete this activity individually or in pairs. Ask them to examine each illustration and decide and discuss what they think is happening in each picture. (The third and fourth illustrations are left somewhat ambiguous, to show the students that people may interpret things in different ways.)

Extension

Ask the students to decide 'What happens next?' for one of the drawings.

EVALUATION

When evaluating, students offer original ideas regarding the success of stimulus material in certain requisite criteria, demonstrating their understanding of the criteria given. Original evaluation illustrates complete engagement and synthesis of the subject matter. Students also display confidence and certainty in their own judgements, valuing their own opinion as much as any other. An ability to measure success will aid a student in all walks of life, as they are able to challenge the idea of fixed meaning and create informed personal judgements.

Thumbs up, thumbs down

This activity is a quick and easy introduction to the concept of offering a personal evaluation. The students can see that they do not always have to share the same views.

 Group size: Individual

 Time: 10 minutes

 Resources: Paper and pencils. For a class of 30, display the following information:

A: 0–10   **B:** 10–20   **C:** 20+

(Change the numbers as appropriate to the size of the class)

What to do

Explain that you are going to call out different categories and ask the students to put their thumbs up, down or horizontal to express likes, dislikes or neither. Before each action, they are going to guess how many students will be in the category that you name by writing down A, B or C. In one turn you might ask them to guess how many students will put thumbs up, in another how many will put thumbs down and in a third, how many will choose neither like or dislike. Categories could be who likes ice-cream, swimming, a named pop group, a television programme, cats. Each time a student guesses correctly, they gain a point.

Extension

Put six to eight categories on the board, such as favourite dinner, favourite pet, favourite chocolate bar, favourite sport, favourite television programme, favourite lesson in school. Ask the students to write down their favourites for each category, then ask for a volunteer to stand up. The other students try to guess their favourites and write them down. The volunteer reads out their list and the others get a point for each correct guess.

Desert island

The students evaluate the importance of items to their life.

 Group size: Individual

 Time: 15–20 minutes

 Resources: Paper and pencils

What to do

Explain to the students that they are to be marooned on a desert island. There will be food and drink available and an empty hut to shelter in. They are allowed to take five items from home to the island. They must think of the five items that will be the most valuable to their lifestyle and explain why each is so important to them. When they have finished, ask the students to compare their items. Are there certain things that are universal to most? Looking at their choice of items, can they see one aspect of their life as more important, for example physical comfort, leisure, spiritual or physical health and well-being?

Extension

Ask for volunteers to choose one of their items and make a case for it to the other students. The class then take a vote on the item that they think was best presented.

Town planners

The students have to evaluate the importance of certain buildings and facilities to a community and give their reasons why.

Group size: 5

Time: 20–30 minutes

Resources: Paper and pencils

What to do

Put the students into groups of five. Explain that they represent a town council planning committee. A large, multi-national company wants to build a factory in their town that will create 200 new jobs. Unfortunately, the only suitable sites already contain other buildings or facilities and one of these will have to be destroyed. The students, in role, must choose three sites from the list below in order of preference and say why they have made their choices. Call the groups together to compare their sites and see how much agreement there is on the choices.

A school playing field

A woodland area of outstanding beauty

A park

The leisure centre's astro-turf

An old people's home and grounds

A cut-price supermarket

A bus station

A youth club

A hostel for the homeless

A nursery for toddlers

A football ground.

Extension

Make a shortlist of contenders and take a class vote on their chosen site. They may only vote for one. If there is a tied vote, remove the other contenders and vote again, until one site receives a majority.

Game show

The students evaluate a selection of game shows to decide which they think would be the most successful and why.

Group size: 4–5

Time: 20–30 minutes

Resources: Paper and pencils

What to do

Put the students into groups of four or five. Explain that they are going to devise a television game show for a Saturday night 7.00 pm slot. They must think about the activities involved and how they will appeal to a family audience. Ask for a volunteer from each group to deliver a pitch about their show – saying why they think it should be chosen. The groups then vote on their choice of *another* group's show. If there is a tied vote, continue until there is a clear winner.

Extension

Ask the students to rehearse and act out the winning game show.

Interviews

The students evaluate responses in mock interviews to decide which candidate would be the successful applicant.

Group size: Individual

Time: 30+ minutes

Resources: With the students' help, write up a list of suitable questions that might be asked in a job interview. You can decide the type of position that is being advertised either prior to the lesson or with the students' help.

What to do

Ask for a volunteer to be the boss and ask the questions of the interviewees. Ask for five volunteers to be the interviewees. They take it in turns to be interviewed, but they are not allowed to hear the responses of the other candidates. They must either wait outside the door for their turn or you can arrange for them to be accommodated in a nearby room. When all five have been interviewed, ask them to remain outside while the other students take a vote on who will be the successful candidate. If you don't want the numbers known, ask the students to write down who they have chosen on a slip of paper and count them.

Extension

Without involving the interviewed students' names, discuss what strengths and weaknesses influenced their choices. Take a vote on the characteristic they consider the most important in an interview.

Suitable jobs

The students evaluate a friend's skills and aptitudes to decide which job would most suit them.

Group size: Pairs

Time: 10–15 minutes

Resources: Whiteboard and pen

What to do

Write a list of ten varied jobs on the whiteboard, such as plumber, doctor, hairdresser, shop assistant, architect, mechanic, teacher, fashion designer, gardener, driver. Ask the students to form friendship pairs. Without consulting their partners, the students must decide which of the jobs would be most suitable for their friend and why. When each pair of students has made their decisions, they explain their choices and see if their partner agrees with them.

Variation

This activity can be carried out with other subjects, such as hobbies or dinners.

White bread or brown?

The students are encouraged to give reasons for their evaluations in this activity and compare their reasons to those of other students.

 Group size: 5

 Time: 15–20 minutes

 Resources: Paper and pencils

What to do

Put the students into groups of five. Each member of the group takes a turn at being the leader and asking a comparative question of the others, such as, 'Do you prefer white bread or brown?' 'Do you prefer apples or bananas?' 'Would you rather travel by car or train?' 'Which do you dislike the most, wind or rain?' 'Would you rather be too hot or too cold?' The students write down their preference with a reason for their choice. They get one point if they choose the same as the leader and an additional point if they have given the same reason. If you think that they will find it difficult to think of suitable questions, you can write a selection on the board.

Extension

If you think that the students would be able to provide suitable reasons, try some questions on abstract concepts such as, 'What is most important, honesty or kindness?' 'Which is worse, telling a lie or stealing?' 'Which would you prefer, money or good health?'

Priorities

The students are asked to evaluate and prioritise a list of items in the order that they consider most important for their happiness and well-being.

 Group size: Whole class

 Time: 20–30 minutes

 Resources: For each student, an A4 sheet of paper with one of the following statements written on it in large letters:

Good public transport, feeling safe on the streets, having cool friends, not being bullied, living in a big house, eating healthy food, wearing trendy clothes, having a boy/girlfriend, having a cool mobile phone, having money, being famous, being able to drive, living near good shops, exercise, having a pet, being good at school, being independent, listening to good music, going on the internet, having a hobby, going to university, getting a job, having holidays abroad, going to pop concerts/festivals, having the latest electronic game, watching television.

What to do

Give each student one of the statement sheets and ask them to read out what is written. Ask them to hold their sheets of paper in front of them so that everyone can see all of the statements and then evaluate the statements. Among these statements, what do they consider are the priorities to achieve happiness and well-being as an adult? They must put themselves in a line, going from the most important to the least important statement. Where there is any disagreement, take a class vote.

Extension

Ask the students to choose just three of the statements that are the most important to them and take a vote to find out the top three statements.

First five

The students evaluate a brief excerpt from a film or book to make a judgement of preference, giving reasons for their choice.

Group size: Individual

Time: 20–30 minutes

Resources: Choose five books with interesting first lines or five films

What to do

Either read out the first lines of five different books or watch the first minute or two of five different films. Based on what they have seen or heard, ask the students to put the titles in order of preference, starting with the one they would most like to read/watch, and stating their reasons why. Ask for volunteers to read out their list.

Extension

If you have used books, ask the students to make up a second line for each title. If you have used films, ask the students to choose their favourite and write a brief synopsis of a plot they think would follow on from the opening scene they have watched.

Who's the most important?

The students evaluate the importance of a selection of key workers to everyday life, stating the reasons for their choices.

 Group size: Individual

 Time: 15–20 minutes

 Resources: A list of key workers, such as bin-men, mechanics, policemen, nurses, teachers, electricians, builders, airline pilots, road surfacers, factory workers, shop assistants, members of parliament, fruit pickers, bank assistants

What to do

Ask the students to read through the list and choose the five categories of workers that they consider the most important to maintaining everyday life. They must give reasons for their choices. Ask for volunteers to read their list and the reasons they have identified.

Extension

Work with the whole class to arrange the list in order of importance. Where opinions are divided, you can take a class vote.

Product posters

The students evaluate named categories in advertisements that they have created.

 Group size: Pairs or groups of 3–4

 Time: 20–30 minutes

 Resources: A selection of magazines containing advertisements; paper and pencils; scissors; glue

What to do

Put the students into pairs or small groups. Explain that they are going to produce posters for a product of their choice. As research, they are going to look at the advertisements in the magazines noting their style. When the students have completed their own advertisements, display them and ask the students, in their groups or pairs, to evaluate how successful they consider each poster to be in terms of attracting their target audience, image, copy and colours. Ask the students to vote for their favourite, but they are not allowed to vote for their own poster.

Variation

Put the students into pairs or small groups, each with a magazine advertisement. Ask the students to evaluate their poster commenting on image, copy and colours and how successful they think it would be at attracting the intended target audience.

Making improvements

The students evaluate what constitutes success in a chosen field and consider ways to improve performance.

 Group size: Individual or pairs

 Time: 15–20 minutes

 Resources: Paper and pencils

What to do

Either individually or in pairs, the students are asked to choose a team or individual from the world of sport or entertainment. Ask the students to make a list of all the factors that contribute to their team/person's success and how that success is measured. For example, if they choose a football team, success is measured in goals; if they choose a pop star, success is measured in CD sales or downloads. When the students have completed this activity, ask for volunteers to name their chosen team/person and read out their list. Can the other students think of additional factors that contribute towards their success?

Extension

Ask the students to think of ways in which they could improve their chosen team/person to make them even more successful.

Good or bad?

In this fun activity, students have to think of their own methods of evaluation – the wackier the better.

Group size: Pairs or groups of 3–4

Time: 15–20 minutes

Resources: Paper and pencils

What to do

Talk to the students about the methods of evaluation that we use, for example rating things A, B, C, D, giving marks out of 10, marking levels 4, 5, 6, 7, giving a thumbs up/thumbs down, using symbols such as ticks and crosses. Ask the students what purpose these methods serve: do they rate things or put them into an order? Put the students into pairs or small groups. Ask them to think of a new method of evaluation. Encourage them to use their imaginations and make the method as wacky and interesting as they can. When they have completed the activity, ask the students to explain their methods of evaluation to the class and take a vote to find the most popular. Students cannot vote for their own method.

Extension

Divide the class into three groups and give each group one of the methods thought up by the students. Ask them to use the method to evaluate something. For example they could rate a list of food items on how much they liked them. Ask the students how well the method of evaluation that they used worked. Did they encounter any problems?

Self and peer evaluation

The students complete a list of statements for themselves and a close friend and then check their friend's list to see how correctly they have evaluated their friend's choices.

 Group size: Pairs

 Time: 20–30 minutes

 Resources: For each student, a copy of the photocopiable sheet *Self and peer evaluation* (p. 152)

What to do

Ask the students to pair up with someone they know well. If there is an odd number of students, create a three and allow the students to choose who they will evaluate. Explain that they are going to complete a list of statements for themselves and also they are going to guess the responses that their partner would make and write these down alongside their own. They must not confer while they are doing this. When they have completed their lists, they compare their guesses with their partner's written response. Tell the students that they can award themselves a point for each correct guess.

Extension

Fill in the list of statements and ask the students to work in their pairs to guess your responses.

Critical evaluation

The students are asked to give reasons that support their evaluations of a given statement.

Group size: Individual

Time: 20–30 minutes

Resources: For each student, create an A4 sheet of paper. At the top of each sheet write a different statement. For example: Summer is a nicer season than spring, Cycling is a healthier activity than swimming, Apples are tastier than oranges, Ice-cream is nicer than chocolate, History is more interesting than geography, Watching a film is better than reading a book, A holiday in the sun is better than a holiday in the snow.

What to do

Give each student one of the sheets. Ask them to write down whether they agree/disagree with the statement at the top, giving reasons and putting their name, and then pass the paper on to another student. They continue in this way until the sheets of paper are full on both sides. So, for example a sheet might have the statement 'Summer is a nicer season than spring' and underneath comments such as 'I agree with the statement because summer is usually drier and hotter and I like the sun. Jared' followed by 'I disagree with Jared because summer can also be wet and I like to see all the leaves and flowers coming out in Spring. Shoniece'. Ask the students to take turns to read out the statements and the comments underneath.

Variation

If you prefer, you can ask the students to write their own statement at the top of the sheets of paper. Encourage them to think of something that they feel strongly about.

PHOTOCOPIABLE RESOURCES

What makes a rainbow?

1. What two things do you need to make a rainbow?

2. Which two colours combine to create 'green'?

3. Give two functions of the roots of a plant.

4. Give three ingredients of pastry.

5. Name three countries in Europe.

6. What is 'toad in the hole' made from?

7. Which is the odd one out and why: Geranium, Hellebore, Marsupial, Daffodil?

8. What is wrong about the following statement: 'As I ate my lunch I looked out of the window and saw a tawny owl'?

9. What are the three main ingredients of sponge cake?

10. Which is the odd one out and why: alpha, beta, wonga, gamma?

11. Think of three words that have the Latin word for 100 as their root.

12. What two elements make water?

13. Where would you suffer from 'altitude sickness' and why?

14. What is wrong with the following statement: 'At the North Pole I saw polar bears and penguins'?

15. Might Charles Dickens have eaten dinner with William Shakespeare?

16. Could you travel by train from Liverpool to Dublin?

17. Which is the odd one out and why: Julius Caesar, Augustus, Ghengis Khan, Nero?

18. In what part of the body is the larynx?

19. What is wrong with the following statement: 'I looked through the telescope and saw the rings around Jupiter'?

20. Name three famous things associated with China.

Ingredients

casserole	onions	carrots	beef	peas	gravy
cake	flour	eggs	sugar	jam	icing
ploughman's	roll	butter	cheese	pickle	pickled onions
salad	ham	lettuce	tomatoes	cucumber	celery
trifle	jelly	sponge fingers	raspberries	custard	cream

Stages of life

Jaques: All the world's a stage,
And all the men and women merely players;
They have their exits and their entrances:
And one man in his time plays many parts,
His acts being seven ages. At first, the infant,
Muling and puking in the nurse's arms.
Then, the whining school boy, with his satchel,
And shining morning face, creeping like a snail
Unwillingly to school. And then, the lover,
Sighing like furnace, with a woeful ballad
Made to his mistress' eyebrow. Then, a soldier,
Full of strange oaths, and bearded like the pard,
Jealous in honour, sudden and quick in quarrel,
Seeking the bubble reputation
Even in the cannon's mouth. And then, the justice,
In fair round belly, with good capon lin'd,
With eyes severe, and beard of formal cut,
Full of wise saws and modern instances:
And so he plays his part. The sixth age shifts
Into the lean and slipper'd pantaloon,
With spectacles on nose, and pouch on side;
His youthful hose well sav'd, a world too wide
For his shrunk shank; and his big manly voice
Turning again toward childish treble, pipes
And whistles in his sound. Last scene of all,
That ends this strange eventful history,
Is second childishness, and mere oblivion:
Sans teeth, sans eyes, sans taste, sans everything.

Shapes

What's been added?

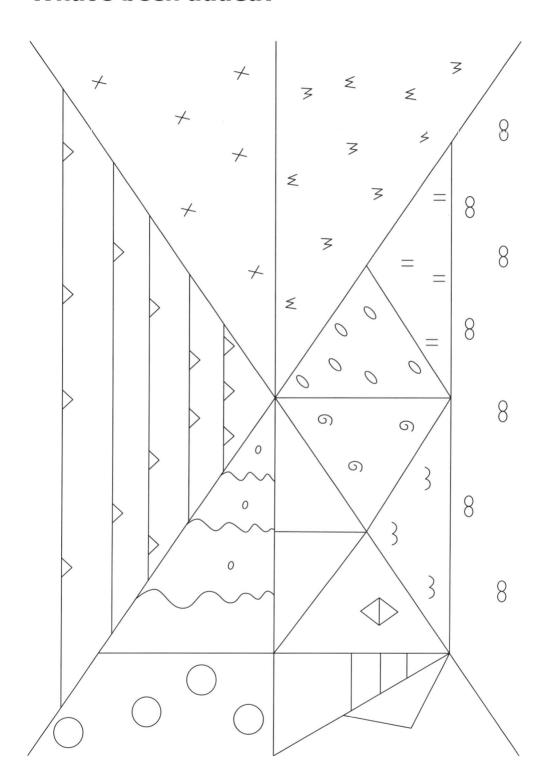

Headlines

ALIENS LANDED IN MY BEDROOM

I WAS TRAPPED ON A RUNAWAY CAMEL

I WENT SWIMMING AND AN OCTOPUS STUCK TO MY FACE

I JUMPED FROM A MOVING TRAIN

I CYCLED DOWN MOUNT EVEREST WITHOUT ANY BRAKES

I WENT OVER NIAGARA FALLS IN A CANOE

I HAD A JUMPING COMPETITION WITH A KANGAROO

I WENT SWIMMING WITH SHARKS WITH NO GOGGLES

I WAS MISTAKEN FOR A DANGEROUS SPY

I WAS LOST IN A PITCH BLACK UNDERGROUND TUNNEL

WHEN THE QUEEN VISITED OUR TOWN, I ACCIDENTALLY KNOCKED
HER OVER

I DISCOVERED A TALKING MOUSE

A WITCH TURNED ME INTO A FROG

I HAD A WRESTLING MATCH WITH A BEAR

MY CAR TURNED INTO CHITTY-CHITTY-BANG-BANG AND FLEW UP
INTO THE AIR

I FOUND A DINOSAUR IN MY GARDEN

A VAMPIRE CAME TO MY HOUSE FOR DINNER

A CROCODILE WAS IN MY SWIMMING POOL

EVERYTHING I TOUCHED BECAME INVISIBLE

I FELL DOWN A HOLE AND CAME OUT IN AUSTRALIA

Where do we belong?

Hospital	Theatre	Church	Ship	Office
bed-pan	stage	altar	cabin	desk
syringe	curtains	aisle	port-hole	shredder
surgical tape	backdrop	belfry	engine room	photocopier
X-ray	props	pew	funnel	filing cabinet
stethoscope	orchestra pit	organ	sextant	computer
scalpel	dressing room	Bible	anchor	paper clip

Going round

Dentist	*Dentist's patient*
Can you show me which tooth is hurting?	It's this tooth at the back.
Doctor	*Doctor's patient*
Do you need more heart tablets?	Yes, it's still beating irregularly.
Hairdresser	*Hairdresser's client*
Do you like conditioner?	No, it makes my hair greasy.
Baker	*Baker's customer*
Do you want your usual loaf?	Yes, and two cream buns please.
Fish and chip shop proprietor	*Fish and chip customer*
Do you want salt and vinegar?	Just salt and a sachet of ketchup.
Window cleaner	*Window cleaner's customer*
Shall I wash the windows inside as well?	Just wash them outside today please.
Taxi driver	*Taxi driver's client*
Where do you want me to drive you?	Take me to 25 South Road, please.
Policeman	*Suspect*
Did you steal the valuable painting?	Officer, I swear I'm innocent.
Gardener	*Gardener's client*
Shall I prune the roses today?	No, turn the compost heap please.
Fish shop owner	*Fish shop customer*
Would you like some fresh herrings?	No, I'll take a rainbow trout.

Jeweller	*Jeweller's customer*
Do you want a diamond ring?	I prefer rubies or emeralds.
Train conductor	*Train passenger*
Can I see your ticket please?	Here it is, I'm going to Bath.
Plane stewardess	*Airplane passenger*
Is your belt fastened for take-off?	Help me please, I hate flying.
Butcher	*Butcher's customer*
Did you want a leg of lamb?	No, I'll have some pork chops.
Teacher	*Pupil*
Have you handed in your book?	I haven't finished the homework.
Shoe-shop owner	*Shoe-shop customer*
What size shoe do you take?	I think I'm a size 40 foot.
Bank clerk	*Bank customer*
How would you like the money?	I'll have £10 notes please.
Restaurant waiter	*Restaurant customer*
Have you decided on your meal?	I'd like steak and chips please.
Painter and decorator	*Painter's customer*
Shall I paint the walls green?	I'd rather have cream walls.
Ice cream salesman	*Ice cream customer*
What flavour ice-cream do you want?	I'll have strawberry flavour.

Fire burn and cauldron bubble

Scene I

A dark cave. In the middle, a boiling cauldron.
Thunder. Enter the three Witches.

1 Witch   Thrice the brinded cat hath mew'd.

2 Witch   Thrice and once the hedge-pig whin'd.

3 Witch   Harpier cries: 'Tis time, 'tis time.

1 Witch   Round about the cauldron go:

In the poison entrails throw. –

Toad, that under cold stone

Days and nights has thirty-one

Swelter'd venom, sleeping got,

Boil thou first i'the charmed pot.

All   Double, double, toil and trouble:

Fire, burn; and, cauldron, bubble.

2 Witch   Fillet of a fenny snake,

In the cauldron boil and bake;

Eye of newt, and toe of frog,

Wool of bat, and tongue of dog,

Adder's fork, and blind-worm's sting,

Lizard's leg, and howlet's wing,

For a charm of powerful trouble,

Like a hell-broth boil and bubble.

All   Double, double toil and trouble,

Fire, burn; and cauldron, bubble.

3 Witch   Scale of dragon, tooth of wolf;

Witches' mummy; maw, and gulf,

Of the ravin'd salt-sea shark:

Root of hemlock, digg'd i'the dark;

Liver of blaspheming Jew;

Gall of goat, and slips of yew,

Sliver'd in the moon's eclipse;

Nose of Turk, and Tartar's lips;

Finger of birth-strangled babe,

Ditch-deliver'd by a drab,

Make the gruel thick and slab:

And thereto a tiger's chaudron,

For the ingredients of our cauldron.

All   Double, double toil and trouble:

Fire, burn, and, cauldron, bubble.

2 Witch   Cool it with a baboon's blood;

Then the charm is firm and good.

What's my line?

1.

'Another busy day ahead. I've several visits to make before I get to base. Old Mrs Morris tells me about her granddaughter's wedding as I hold her hand. She's looking remarkably well for 85. Mrs Patel tells me all about her baby's red rash and how he's very fretful – I expect he's just teething, but I take his temperature anyway. Back at base, a dozen hopeful faces look at me as I walk through to my room. Someone has a very nasty cough – sounds like bronchitis – I'll have to prescribe antibiotics. I hope everyone else doesn't catch it.'

2.

'I drive past the park for the fifth time that day. I wish I was out there sitting in the cool shade of a tree. The sun beats down through the large windscreen and I am so hot. I stop at the church, passengers get on, then I'm off again. Traffic's bad today. There's roadworks on my route and my vehicle is large and not easy to turn. Behind me, people sit in pairs and chatter or listen to music on their headphones.'

3.

'I'm hoping the rain holds off long enough to do the mowing. The roses are covered in greenfly – a wash with a weak soapy solution, I think, will cure that. I prop the spade against the wall. The hole's big enough for the root ball of this sapling. Looks like there'll be a good crop of redcurrants this year.'

Mimes

I can't read a book so I put on my glasses.

I put down the cat's dish of food and stroke the cat.

I put on my dance Wii™ and start dancing.

I throw and catch a ball with a friend.

I make a cup of tea and drink it.

I wipe the dog's feet after a muddy walk.

I take a dog for a walk on a lead.

I put sugar, flour and eggs into a bowl and mix them together for a cake.

I slice cheese for a sandwich.

I drop a cup that breaks, then sweep up the pieces.

I dig up a plant in the garden.

I put a pizza in the microwave and switch it on.

I put on my make-up in front of a mirror.

I hammer a picture hook into a wall and hang a picture on it.

I write a letter on my computer.

I plug in my vacuum cleaner and vacuum my carpet.

Quick thinking

Professor Clumber and Dirk Didgery had completed their latest invention. It had been a race against their rivals, Mo Clutterbucks and Irving Nosebag, to produce a robotic machine that could wash and polish a car. They stood back to admire their invention, unaware that Sam Slipperyeel, their rival's spy, was watching them through a small window at the back of the building. Sam Slipperyeel was as slippery as his name suggests and he had sabotage on his mind. He intended to burn down the building as soon as the inventors had left and destroy their prototype. He had seen off Mo and Irving's rivals on numerous occasions. They had included Brad Loxley and his egg-peeler, Majarupee Sonar and her cat flea detector, Dr. Handlebar and his computerised moustache trimmer and, last but not least, Professor Stinkhorn and his amazing feet-tickling machine (to cheer people up when they were sad). Their version of this last invention had earned Clumber and Didgery a fortune and they had passed a substantial sum on to Sam. So, now Sam watched and waited for his opportunity to destroy this latest trial model, before it was perfected.

Questions

1. Which sentence in the text has the most words?

2. How many people are named in the text?

3. Which is the longest surname?

4. How many S's are there in the sentence that begins 'Sam Slipperyeel was as slippery ...'

5. How many times is Sam mentioned in the text?

6. Put the surnames into alphabetical order.

7. Who invented the moustache trimmer?

8. How many times does the word 'and' appear in the text?

9. Does the sentence 'Their version of this last ...' have more or fewer S's than the 'Sam Slipperyeel ...' sentence?

10. What word in the text has the same meaning as 'trial model'?

Making sense

Theoldmanlikedeatinggreenappleswhiledrinkingacupoftea.

What colour was the food he liked to eat?

Iorderedfourburgersthreeportionsofchipstwocolasanapplejuiceandacoffee.

How many drinks were mentioned altogether?

Thefilmwasanactionpackedblockbusterandthemaincharacterwasanunder-covercop.

What was the main part?

Thelionesswascreepinguponthezebrainthelonggrasswaitingtopounce.

What was in danger of being attacked?

ZacthrewtheballforMutttochasebutthedogwasmoreinterestedinsniffin-goutarabbithole.

What smell attracted the dog?

TheplanewascomingintolandIlookedoutofthewindowandsawtheseabelow-Icouldseethetinyboatsonthewaterandasmallislandcoveredintrees.

What was on the water?

Thefireroaredthroughthebuildingandthickgreysmokepouredoutofeverywin-dowtheheatwasterribleandeverynowandthenIheardahugeexplosion.

What was coming out of the windows?

Put together

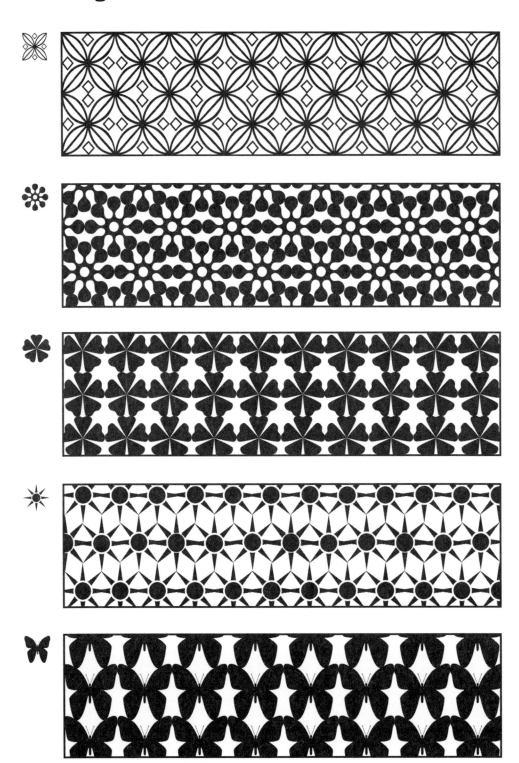

How many?

How many?

1. What instrument is the busker playing?

2. How many tea-pots are displayed in the shop window?

3. How many carrier bags is the lady in the fur gilet carrying?

4. What is the lady in the spotty dress carrying?

5. What is the child putting into the rubbish bin?

6. Describe the head-gear of the girl wearing stripy trousers.

7. How many people are carrying bags?

8. What has the man who has fallen over dropped?

9. What is sitting on top of the modern sculpture?

10. How many people are wearing their hair in a pony-tail?

11. What has the man who is talking on his mobile got on the front of his sweatshirt?

12. What garment is a lady holding up to show her husband?

13. How many wheels can you see?

14. Where is the lost teddy?

15. How many spots does the man wearing the bobble hat have on his jumper?

16. What are the identical twins carrying in their hands?

17. What is the man with the moustache holding?

18. Who has dropped an ice-cream on the floor?

19. Which shop is having a half price sale?

20. What is the man with the sandwich board advertising?

Which line is longer?

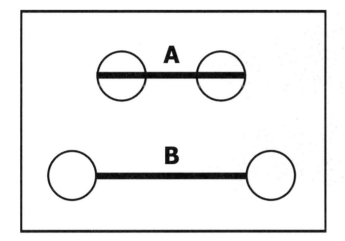

Which line is longer,
A or B?

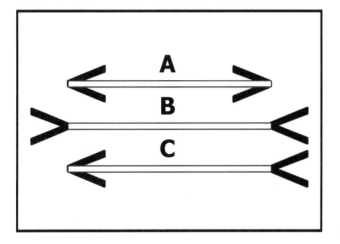

Which line is longer,
A, B or C?

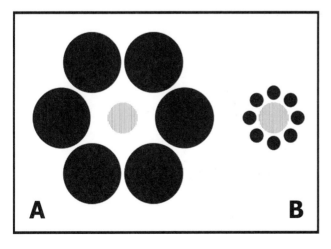

Which of the pale
grey circles is larger,
A or B?

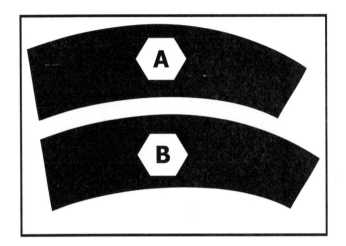

Which shape is larger, A or B?

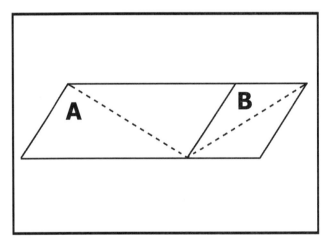

Which dotted line is longer, A or B?

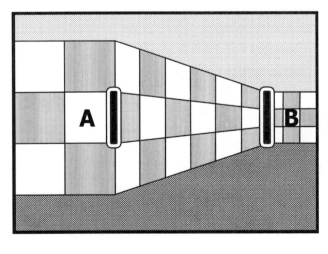

Which thick black line is longer, A or B?

What do you see?

Interpret the letter

Paint splodge

Fortune cards

Silent movie sequences

1. Two people are travelling in a car and it breaks down. One of them walks to a house nearby and asks the occupant if they could use the phone to telephone for help. A mechanic arrives and fixes the car.

2. Three children take a picnic into the woods. They set out their picnic on the ground and begin to eat. A wasp buzzes around and stings one of the children. They grab the picnic items and run off. They are met by an adult who treats the sting with a spray.

3. Four people are in a boat. They start to mess around and one person falls into the water. A second person jumps in to help them swim back to the boat. The remaining two people help them both back into the boat.

4. A customer is talking to a bank clerk. Two robbers burst in and demand money. The clerk hands over the cash and the robbers make their escape.

5. Two children are trapped in a house on fire. Their mother is outside in a panic begging for someone to help. She tries to re-enter the house, but the flames are too fierce and drive her back. Using a ladder, a neighbour rescues the children from an upstairs bedroom of the house.

6. A surprise party has been arranged for someone. The party-goers hide and wait for the birthday boy/girl to arrive, then spring out with their surprise.

7. A couple are mountain climbing. One falls and breaks a leg. The other climber contacts mountain rescue and explains what has happened. Two rescuers arrive to take the injured person to safety.

8. Someone is being chased by two enemies. They try to hide in various places, but are discovered and continue to flee. Eventually, they are taken in and hidden by someone.

What's the book?

1. I stood behind a tree and watched the window. They entered the room shortly after and I got a good look at both of them. I adjusted my ear-piece and I could hear them talking, loud and clear.

2. The Loire Valley is sometimes called the 'Garden of France' because of its vineyards and the fruit and vegetables grown there. It is notable for its historic towns and chateaux.

3. Pre-heat the oven to Gas Mark 4. Place all the ingredients into a bowl and whisk thoroughly for 2 minutes.

4. During training, it is advisable to keep a few treats in your pocket. These can be used, for example, as a reward when training to sit and stay or to walk to heel.

5. Once upon a time, in the far off land of Scrimalgia, there lived a mean and terrible ogre.

6. The trees around are white with snow,
The ground untouched for far ahead.
And I do not know where I go,
For 'tis a long way from my bed.

7. In 1453 the long warfare between France and England, which had begun with the battle of Sluys in 1340 in the reign of Edward III, came to an end, leaving only the city of Calais in English hands.

8. CHARLOCK Medium/tall, roughly hairy annual. Lower leaves large, lobed and toothed. Flowers yellow, 15–20mm, April–October.

Letters from?

1.

> Dear
>
> From the symptoms you describe, I think you may have tonsillitis and you will need a course of antibiotics.
>
> Yours sincerely

2.

> Dear
>
> Thank you so much for the parcel, it was just what I wanted. I hope Uncle Dan is well.
>
> Love from

3.

> Hi
>
> I think you'll like their music so let me know today or all the tickets might be sold.
>
> LOL

4.

> To
>
> If you know what's good for you, you'll hand it in before you leave.
>
> Signed:

5.

Dear

This place is fantastic, so much to do and see. Amazing views and great food.

Miss you

6.

Dear

I am hoping to be out on Wednesday. Everything seems to be going well and I am up and about now.

See you soon

7.

Hi

Come and join us for the weekend. It will be so much fun. There will be clues to follow and lots of twists and turns to unravel. There's a prize for the person who guesses correctly.

:)

8.

Dear

Thank you for your support so far. Every contribution helps to provide for basic needs and save lives. We hope that you will continue to help our cause.

With best wishes

Check out the scene

Self and peer evaluation

	Self	Partner
1. My favourite lesson at school is		
2. My favourite colour is		
3. My favourite dinner is		
4. I am really good at		
5. My favourite leisure activity is		
6. My favourite sport is		
7. My favourite item of clothing is		
8. My favourite season is		
9. My favourite film is		
10. I am a night/morning person		
11. I would rather have health/wealth		
12. I would rather be hot/cold		
13. I prefer to travel by plane/boat		
14. I would rather eat chips/salad		
15. I would rather have cake/chocolate		
16. I would rather have a Mars/Aero bar		
17. I would rather watch a film/play on a DS™		
18. I would rather watch skating/skiing		
19. I would rather drink apple/orange juice		
20. I prefer an elephant/tiger		